9/03

D1216744

The High Price of Materialism

The High Price of Materialism

Tim Kasser

A Bradford Book
The MIT Press
Cambridge, Massachusetts
London, England

The summary of *The Rainbow Fish,* by Marcus Pfister, is printed by permission of North-South Books.

This book was set in Sabon by Achorn Graphic Services, Inc. and was printed and bound in the United States of America.

Library of Congress Cataloging-in-Publication Data

Kasser, Tim.
 The high price of materialism / Tim Kasser.
  p. cm.
 Includes bibliographical references and index.
 ISBN 0-262-11268-X (alk. paper)
  1. Acquisitiveness. 2. Avarice. 3. Materialism—Psychological aspects. 4. Happiness. 5. Conduct of life. I. Title.

BF698.35.A36 K37   2002
302′.17—dc21

2002016506

To the doctors, nurses, researchers, and staff
at St. Jude Children's Research Hospital in Memphis, Tennessee,
and the Midwest affiliate in Peoria, Illinois

Contents

Foreword

At this point in human history we have enough material resources to feed, clothe, shelter, and educate every living individual on Earth. Not only that: we have at the same time the global capacity to enhance health care, fight major diseases, and considerably clean up the environment. That such resources exist is not merely a utopian fantasy, it is a reality about which there is little serious debate.

Nonetheless, a quick look around most any part of this warming globe tells us just how far we are from achieving any of these goals. If we hold our eyes wide open we can see that the human community is instead dividing itself into two distinct worlds: a "first" world filled with opulence, luxury, and material excess; and a "third" world characterized by deprivation, poverty, and struggle. Whereas first and third worlds could formerly be distinguished along national boundaries, increasingly, and in most countries, one finds relatively insulated pockets of wealth surrounded by ever widening fields of impoverishment. Most of the world's population is now growing up in winner-take-all economies, where the main goal of individuals is to get whatever they can for themselves: to each according to his greed. Within this economic landscape, selfishness and materialism are no longer being seen as moral problems, but as cardinal goals of life.

This global reality exists, however, only because people, and I mean each one of us, can so readily be converted to the religions of consumerism and materialism. Indeed, such mass conversion seems already to have occurred. Vast numbers of us have been seduced into believing that having more wealth and material possessions is essential to the good life. We have swallowed the idea that, to be well, one first has to be well-off. And many of us, consciously or unconsciously, have learned to evaluate our own well-being and accomplishment not by looking inward at our spirit or integrity, but by looking outward at what we have and what we can buy. Similarly, we have adopted a world view in which the worth and success of others is judged not by their apparent wisdom, kindness, or community contributions, but in terms of whether they possess the right clothes, the right car, and more generally, the right "stuff."

Perhaps the most insidious aspect of this modern measure of worth is that it is not simply about having *enough,* but about having *more* than others do. That is, feelings of personal worth are based on how one's pile of money and possessions compares with that of others; both those who surround us in real life and those seen only in the pseudorealities of television and movies. In this context, no one can ever have enough because, aside from Bill Gates, there are always others who have more. Accordingly, at all levels of wealth one can find individuals who crave ever more expensive toys, status symbols, and image builders, and who subjectively feel that they need more than they currently have. As advertising executives have known for decades, we become good consumers only when we experience mere "desires" as urgent "needs," and when our conception of the "necessities" of life becomes ever more blurry and bloated. Clearly, by these criteria, most of us have become good consumers.

It would be one thing if the promises of the consumer society were real, but they are not. And this is where this succinct, but important, book by Tim Kasser comes in. Kasser reviews a formidable body of research that highlights what for most of us is a quite counter-intuitive fact: even when people obtain more money and material goods, they do not become more satisfied with their lives, or more psychologically healthy because of it. More specifically, once people are above poverty levels of income, gains in wealth have little to no incremental payoff in terms of happiness or well-being. However, the central focus of Kasser's treatise, and what makes it new and different, is that merely *aspiring* to have greater wealth or more material possessions is likely to be associated with increased personal unhappiness. He documents that people with strong materialistic values and desires report more symptoms of anxiety, are at greater risk for depression, and experience more frequent somatic irritations than those who are less materialistic. They watch more television, use more alcohol and drugs, and have more impoverished personal relationships. Even in sleep, their dreams seem to be infected with anxiety and distress. Thus, insofar as people have adopted the "American dream" of stuffing their pockets, they seem to that extent to be emptier of self and soul.

Perhaps even more important, Kasser provides one of the fullest explanations available of how these empty promises of consumerism can become deeply anchored in our psyches. His explanation focuses not on the play of macroeconomic forces that drive market consumerism, but on a closer-up view of what leads people to so persistently try psychologically to feed off of material goods and status symbols, even though they do not nourish.

Kasser highlights two reasons why materialism is associated with unhappiness. The first concerns the burdens that materialism places on the human soul. Desires to have more and more material goods drive us into an ever more frantic pace of life. Not only must we work harder, but, once possessing the goods, we have to maintain, upgrade, replace, insure, and constantly manage them. Thus, in the journey of life, materialists end up carrying an ever-heavier load, one that expends the energy necessary for living, loving, and learning—the really satisfying aspects of that journey. Thus materialism, although promising happiness, actually creates strain and stress.

Yet if materialism causes unhappiness, it is also the case that unhappiness "causes" materialism. Kasser shows how enhanced desires or "needs" to have more or consume more are deeply and dynamically connected with feelings of personal insecurity. Materialism, it appears, tends to ripen best among people who feel uncertain about matters of love, self-esteem, competence, or control. Indeed, to many people it appears to offer a solution to these common insecurities and anxieties. Our consumer culture persistently teaches that we can counter insecurity by buying our way to self-esteem and loveworthiness. The pervasive message, passed on in popular media, advertisements, and celebrity modeling, is that we will feel better about ourselves if we are surrounded by symbols of worth—toys that others can admire, clothes and adornments that convey attractiveness, or image products that communicate self-importance and aliveness. Kasser suggests that it is because our psychological insecurities are so easily connected with the promise of self-esteem through buying that the fires of consumption are hotly fueled.

Remarkably, economies focused on consumption appear, in turn, to foster conditions that heighten psychological insecurities, and in this sense they fuel themselves. Children grow up in homes where their parents crave products and possessions. Parents today work more hours outside the home than ever, many to acquire the buying power to obtain yet more and more of the goods that they have been taught they and their children "need." In the meantime, attention to children, intimate time with spouses, availability to be in touch with extended family, and other satisfactions that cannot be bought are pushed to the periphery. Not much time for living remains after the working, spending, and consuming are completed. Yet during this free time, children and adults occupy themselves with mass media bulging with advertisements that entice and promise good feelings ahead. Thus, the cultural climate of consumerism creates the very circumstance where love, control, and esteem are not securely experienced, and in which an ever-present tendency to compare oneself with others is fostered. In this climate, almost everyone is vulnerable to "affluenza," an infectious disease in which one becomes addicted to having.

This is of course the tragic tale of modernity—we are the snakes eating our own tails. Yet, in telling the tale, Kasser not only gathers together hard data to confirm what folk wisdom has always told us—that one cannot buy happiness or well-being—he also addresses how we have so easily been hooked by an opposing belief. He provides a quite compelling and yet succinct psychology of materialism—its inward causes in insecurities regarding basic needs, and its personal consequences in terms of empty, alienated, and misdirected lives.

It is for this reason that this engaging text is also extremely timely. For if we are ever to get a handle on our runaway consumerism and marketeering, the starting place is none other than raised consciousness concerning what we value and work for in this worldly existence. The research Kasser compiles raises serious questions about the benefits of materialistic success for both individuals and society, and he uses it to underscore the hidden costs of the American dream in ways that any reader can apply to his or her own life. Although one can find a plethora of books containing diatribes on the evils of materialism, Kasser places this discussion on a more compelling plane by focusing on what the empirical evidence truly shows about materialism and happiness, and by interpreting that evidence in a way that relates it to everyday experience. He uses extant research to inform, to highlight available choices before us, and to provoke us to choose wisely. Amid the infectious spread of affluenza, Kasser's work promotes mindfulness, which, ultimately, may be the most powerful vaccine of all.

Richard M. Ryan
University of Rochester

Acknowledgments

My interest in materialistic values began while I was a graduate student working with Richard Ryan at the University of Rochester. During those early days, many members of the Rochester Motivation Group gave me a great deal of support and encouragement, including Ed Deci, Cynthia Powelson, Betsy Whitehead, and Geoff Williams. Others who helped me during that time include Al and Clara Baldwin, Arnold Sameroff, and Melvin Zax. Since I have become a professor, several of my students have aided this research project by collecting, coding, entering, and analyzing data. They include Michael Berg, Kristin Lindner, Matthew Pace, Sean Siegel, Neil Torbert, and Christina Wagner.

Work on this book began after Alfie Kohn wrote an article in the *New York Times* about the research Richard Ryan and I had been conducting; many thanks to him for lighting this fire. An agent in New York, Lisa Swayne, read the article and called to ask if I would be interested in writing a book on the topic. Lisa has guided me, with great support and knowledge, through many of the challenges involved. Amy Brandt, then at MIT Press, saw promise in the ideas of the book, and convinced the other editors there to publish it; I thank her. The support of the psychology department at Knox College and of Dean Larry Breitborde was crucial in helping me find the time to write. Thanks also to Diana Beck for her encouragement and to everyone at MIT Press for their comments.

Several friends and colleagues read early drafts of this manuscript and provided very helpful advice. Thanks to David Karczynski and Kei Kawashima for giving me the "student view"; Kirk Warren Brown, Allen Kanner, Jeremy Paul Hunter and Ken Sheldon for their thoughtful comments; and the Rev. Lane Andrist, Mary Grow, Mary Jane Kasser, and

Alexis Scudder for helping make the book more accessible to those who are not social scientists. My father, Jim Kasser, was particularly indispensable in this regard, and I thank him for the many hours he devoted to editing this manuscript.

I would especially like to thank four colleagues and good friends for their contributions. Rich Ryan deserves accolades for his patience with me and for giving shape, both empirically and theoretically, to the findings reported here. My collaborations with Ken Sheldon are continually clarifying my thinking about goals and values, and about how they relate to people's lives. My understanding of how materialism and society interact was expanded through the ideas, questions, and critiques of my Knox College student Shivani Khanna. Finally, my wife, Virginia, has for many years helped me think through many different aspects of the argument and research studies presented here, and I thank her for her love and support.

1
Mixed Messages

Chase after money and security
And your heart will never unclench.
Care about people's approval
And you will be their prisoner.
Do your work, then step back.
The only path to serenity.[1]

Twenty-five centuries ago, the Chinese philosopher Lao Tzu penned these six lines, warning people of the dangers of materialistic values. Sages from almost every religious and philosophical background have similarly insisted that focusing on attaining material possessions and social renown detracts from what is meaningful about life.[2] Although we may nod our heads in recognition of this ancient wisdom, such advice is largely drowned out by today's consumeristic hubbub of messages proclaiming that material pursuits, accumulation of things, and presentation of the "right" image provide real worth, deep satisfactions, and a genuinely meaningful life. Newspaper headlines exalt the local lottery winner. Get-rich-quick books climb to the tops of best-seller lists. Multicolor ads flash on Web pages. Celebrities on television hawk everything from sport utility vehicles to mascara. Although they differ in form, each of these messages essentially proclaims "Happiness can be found at the mall, on the Internet, or in the catalogue."

Both types of messages about the value of materialism coexist in contemporary life, and it can be difficult to know whether to follow the sages or the celebrities. Who is right? Will the pursuit of money and possessions bring about "the good life"? Or are the promises of consumer society false?

It seems that wherever we inquire about the value of materialism, we receive conflicting answers. We can ask the government, but while politicians worry that popular consumer culture has displaced community and family values, economic considerations play an overwhelmingly central role in the decisions of most elected officials. We can turn to religious leaders, but while the Bible says that a person who cares about wealth will have trouble entering the kingdom of heaven, televangelists with toothy smiles pull in millions of dollars contributed by their viewers. We can ask wealthy people, but while John Jacob Astor III bemoans, "Money brings me nothing but a certain dull anxiety," Malcolm Forbes replies, "Money isn't everything, as long as you have enough." We can ask the poets, but while Robert Graves writes "There's no poetry in money," Wallace Stevens says "Money is a kind of poetry."[3]

If we turn to psychology for answers we find that it is similarly ambivalent about materialistic values.[4] On the one hand, much of the work conducted by evolutionary and behavioral psychologists is quite compatible with the notion that attainment of wealth and status is of great importance. Evolution-based theories, such as that of David Buss, suggest that the desire to be perceived as wealthy, attractive, and of high status may be built into our genes, as these characteristics (like an opposable thumb or a large forebrain) enabled our ancestors to survive.[5] Similarly, behavioral theories, such as B. F. Skinner's and Albert Bandura's, hold that the successful attainment of external rewards is a motivator of all behavior, and indeed fundamental to individuals' adaptation to society.[6] The behaviorist idea that happiness and satisfaction come from attaining wealth and possessions is exemplified by the fact that the founder of American behaviorism, John Watson, took the basic psychological principles of learning and applied them to advertising on Madison Avenue, a model since followed by thousands of psychologists.[7]

Although behavioral and evolutionary theories largely dominated American academic psychology in the last century, humanistic and existential thinkers such as Carl Rogers, Abraham Maslow, and Erich Fromm voiced a sharply contrasting opinion about the worth of materialistic pursuits. Although they acknowledged the fact that some level of material comfort is necessary to provide for humans' basic physical needs, these psychologists proposed that a focus on materialistic values detracts from well-being and happiness.[8] Humanistic and existential psychologists tend to place qualities such as authentic self-expression, intimate relationships, and contribution to the community at the core of their notions of psychological health. From their viewpoint, a strong focus on materialistic pursuits not only distracts people from experiences conducive to psychological growth and health, but signals a fundamental alienation from what is truly meaningful. For example, when spouses spend most of their time working to make money, they neglect opportunities to be with each other and do what most interests them. No matter how many fancy designer clothes, cars, or jewels they might obtain, no matter how big their house or how up-to-date their electronic equipment, the lost opportunity to engage in pleasurable activities and enjoy each others' companionship will work against need satisfaction, and thus against psychological health.

Given the obviously different sets of predictions about materialism proffered by psychological theories and societal messages, one might expect to find a substantial body of empirical research on this subject. But when I began studying the topic in the early 1990s, I was surprised by the paucity of attempts to bring the scientific method to bear on materialistic values. Certainly there existed substantial social criticism of consumer society and anecdotal evidence regarding the problems of materialistic values. Yet most of the research I found attempted to understand the place of materialism in people's lives by examining how wealth was associated with happiness and psychological adjustment. The basic question behind this research was, "Does money buy happiness?" In answer, psychologists David Myers and Ed Diener wrote:

People have not become happier over time as their cultures have become more affluent. Even though Americans earn twice as much in today's dollars as they did in 1957, the proportion of those telling surveyors from the National Opinion Research Center that they are "very happy" has declined from 35 to 29 percent. Even very rich people—those surveyed among *Forbes* magazine's 100 wealthiest Americans—are only slightly happier than the average American. Those whose income has increased over a 10-year period are not happier than those whose income is stagnant. Indeed, in most nations the correlation between income and happiness is negligible—only in the poorest countries, such as Bangladesh and India, is income a good measure of emotional well-being. Are people in rich countries happier, by and large, than people in not so rich countries? It appears in general they are, but the margin may be slim . . . Furthermore, . . . it is impossible to tell whether the happiness of people in wealthier nations is based on money or is a by-product of other felicities.[9]

Research on the happiness of wealthy and poor people makes it clear that how much we have bears relatively little relationship to our well-being, beyond the point of ensuring sufficient food, shelter, and clothing to survive. Although this is important information, my view is that an inquiry into materialism must go further. To understand fully its impact on people's lives, we must explore how materialistic wants relate to well-being. Because society tells us repeatedly that money and possessions will make us happy, and that they are significant goals for which we should strive, we often organize our lives around pursuing them. But what happens to our well-being when our desires and goals to attain wealth and accumulate possessions become prominent? What happens to our internal experience and interpersonal relationships when we adopt the messages of consumer culture as personal beliefs? What happens to the quality of our lives when we value materialism?

2

Personal Well-Being

To continue much longer overwhelmed by business cares and with most of my thoughts wholly upon the way to make money in the shortest time must degrade me beyond hope of permanent recovery.
—Andrew Carnegie[1]

In recent years, scientific investigators working in a variety of fields have begun to tally the costs of a materialistic lifestyle. Although the body of empirical literature on materialism is not large, especially compared with what we know about topics such as depression, stereotyping, neurons, and memory, its findings are quite consistent. Indeed, what stands out across the studies is a simple fact: people who strongly value the pursuit of wealth and possessions report lower psychological well-being than those who are less concerned with such aims.

Research from Our Lab

Since 1993 my colleagues and I have been publishing a series of papers in which we have been exploring how people's values and goals relate to their well-being. Our focus has been on understanding what people view as important or valuable in life, and on associating those values statistically with a variety of other aspects of their lives, such as happiness, depression, and anxiety. What people value clearly varies from one individual to another. For some, spirituality and religion are of paramount importance; for others, home life, relationships, and family are especially valued; other people focus on having fun and excitement, and others on contributing to the community.[2] In our work, we have been particularly interested in individuals for whom materialistic values are relatively important. That is, compared with other things that might be deemed central to one's life, what happens psychologically when a person feels that making money and having possessions are relatively high in the pantheon of values?

Our First Study

To obtain an answer to this question, Richard Ryan and I began by developing a questionnaire to measure people's values, which we called the Aspiration Index.[3] People who complete this questionnaire are presented with many different types of goals and asked to rate each one in terms of whether it is not at all important, somewhat important, extremely important, and so on. The current version of the Aspiration Index includes a large number of possible goals people might have, such as desires to feel safe and secure, to help the world be a better place, to have a great sex life, and to have good relationships with others. By assessing different types of goals, we can obtain a valid assessment of how important materialistic values are in the context of a person's entire system of values. Most value researchers view this as crucial and insist that we can know how much someone values a particular outcome only when that value is considered in relation to other things that might possibly be valued.[4]

Table 2.1 shows items used to assess materialistic values in our first study. Of central interest, participants reported how important several *financial success* aspirations were to them. We also asked participants how much they were concerned with *self-acceptance* (desires for psycho-

Table 2.1
Financial success items from Kasser and Ryan's (1993) Aspiration Index

---

You will buy things just because you want them.
You will be financially successful.
You will be your own boss.
You will have a job with high social status.
You will have a job that pays well.

Participants rate how important these aspirations are, from not at all to very important.
Reprinted by permission of the American Psychological Association.

logical growth, autonomy, and self-esteem), *affiliation* (desires for a good family life and friendships), and *community feeling* (desires to make the world a better place through one's own actions). From these ratings, we could determine how important, or central, the value of financial success was for each person relative to the other three values.

Ryan and I administered the Aspiration Index to a group of individuals who, second to white rats, form the backbone of much scientific research in psychology: college students. Three hundred sixteen students at the University of Rochester completed a survey packet that included the index and four questionnaires that assessed positive feelings of well-being and negative feelings of distress.

The first measure of well-being assessed self-actualization, a concept made popular by the father of humanistic psychology, Abraham Maslow. Maslow conceived of self-actualization as the pinnacle of psychological health, the state attained by people motivated by growth, meaning, and aesthetics, rather than by insecurity and the attempt to fit in with what other people expect.[5] People who score high on this measure of self-actualization generally agree with statements such as, "It is better to be yourself than to be popular," and "I do not feel ashamed of any of my emotions." Our second measure of well-being, vitality, also assesses psychological growth and the energy that goes along with authentically expressing who one really is. Vital people are likely to feel energized, alert, and overflowing with that wonderful feeling of being alive.

The last two measures assessed two of the most common psychological disorders: depression and anxiety. The depression questionnaire asked participants how frequently they had experienced common depressive symptoms such as feeling down, feeling lonely or disconnected from others, having sleep or appetite troubles, and having little energy or difficulty concentrating. The anxiety measure asked how much they generally experienced nervousness or shakiness inside, felt tense or fearful, or were suddenly scared for no reason.[6]

When we used statistical analyses to examine how people's value orientations related to their well-being, the results were intriguing. Compared with students who were more oriented toward self-acceptance, affiliation, or community feeling, those who considered financial success a relatively central value reported significantly lower levels of self-actualization and vitality, as well as significantly higher levels of depression and anxiety. Notably, such a strong focus was associated with decreased psychological well-being regardless of whether participants were men or women.

These results supported the premise that materialistic values are unhealthy, but we wanted to see if they would be replicated with young adults who were not in college, and with other ways of assessing well-being besides questionnaires. We therefore gave a somewhat shorter version of the Aspiration Index to a wide-ranging group of 140 eighteen-year-olds. These adolescents varied greatly in terms of race, socioeconomic status, and their mothers' psychological health. Their current situation in life was also diverse, with some having dropped out of high school and others going on to college, some already having had children, and others in trouble with the law.

We evaluated psychological well-being in a somewhat different way in this sample. Instead of completing questionnaires, participants met with an experienced clinical psychologist who interviewed them using a set of standard questions. From these interviews ratings were made of the extent to which the teens were socially productive and of how much they exhibited symptoms of behavior disorders. A socially productive adolescent was defined as someone who was doing well in school, was holding down a job, and had hobbies and other outside interests. Behavior disorders, one of the most common of all childhood problems, involved a variety of symptoms expressing oppositional, defiant, and antisocial behavior common in unhappy teens, such as fighting, belonging to a gang, stealing, and torturing small animals. We also measured the teens' general functioning in life by rating them on a 100-point scale commonly used to assess people's level of psychiatric impairment and overall adaptation to life.[7]

Even with these differences in samples and the way we assessed well-being, the results with these teenagers revealed a pattern consistent with our earlier findings: individuals who were focused on financial success, compared with nonmaterialistic values, were not adapting to society well and were acting in rather destructive ways. Specifically, they were not functioning well in school, on the job, or in their extracurricular activities, and were likely to exhibit various symptoms of behavior disorders, such as vandalizing, skipping school, and carrying weapons.

Our first studies therefore showed that when young adults report that financial success is relatively central to their aspirations, low well-being, high distress, and difficulty adjusting to life are also evident. Although we cannot be sure from these results whether materialistic values cause unhappiness, or whether other factors are at work, the results do suggest a rather startling conclusion: the American dream has a dark side, and the pursuit of wealth and possessions might actually be undermining our well-being.

More Recent Work from Our Lab

These results raised a number of further questions in our minds. Were financial success values the only ones that were problematic for people's psychological health? What would happen if we looked at older individuals? Would similar results be found for other aspects of psychological health and distress? These were some of the issues Ryan and I tried to grapple with in our next study.[8]

We began by revising the Aspiration Index to include some other prominent goals and values of consumer culture. Although strivings for money and possessions certainly constitute the core message encouraged by consumeristic and capitalistic cultures, two other goals are also typically encouraged: having the "right" image and being well known socially. Image and fame values are entwined with those for money and possessions in at least a couple of ways. First, the media in consumeristic cultures frequently link these values by having good-looking celebrities sell products. The underlying message is that owning these products will enhance our image and ensure our popularity with others. A second way these values are connected is that image, fame, and money all share a focus of looking for a sense of worth outside of oneself, and involve striving for external rewards and the praise of others. When we focus on these values (which Ryan and I called "extrinsic"), we are seeking sources of satisfaction outside of ourselves, whether in money, in the mirror, or in admiration by others. In capitalistic, consumer cultures such as the United States, these extrinsic values are often encouraged as worthy because they seemingly convey a sense of success and power.

Table 2.2 lists the items we used in the revised version of the Aspiration Index to measure these three types of materialistic values. In several

Table 2.2

Sample items from Kasser and Ryan's (1996) revised Aspiration Index

Financial success

You will have a job with high social status.
You will have a job that pays well.
You will be financially successful.
You will have a lot of expensive possessions.

Social recognition

Your name will be known by many people.
You will do something that brings you much recognition.
You will be admired by many people.
You will be famous.
Your name will appear frequently in the media.

Appealing appearance

You will successfully hide the signs of aging.
You will have people comment often about how attractive you look.
You will keep up with fashions in hair and clothing.
You will achieve the "look" you've been after.
Your image will be one others find appealing.

studies, we have found that people who value one of these values, such as fame, also tend to value money and image. Thus they seem to have "bought into" the prominent goals of consumer society. Notably, this cluster of goals also was found in students from both Russia and Germany, suggesting that the coexistence of money, fame, and image values can be found in cultures less consumeristic than the United States.[9]

Having expanded the Aspiration Index to measure a greater number of values relevant to the messages of consumer culture, Ryan and I set out to determine whether our results would be the same in adults as they were in college students and teenagers. We randomly sampled a group of 100 adults living in a diverse neighborhood of Rochester, New York. The participants ranged from eighteen to seventy-nine years of age and came from lower, middle, and upper socioeconomic backgrounds. The survey packet we left at participants' doors contained the revised Aspiration Index and the four measures of well-being we used previously (self-actualization, vitality, anxiety, depression measures). Participants also reported on their physical health by noting how often they had experienced nine physical symptoms in the past week (headache, stomach aches, backaches, etc.).[10]

The findings largely corroborated those reported with young adults. Adults who focused on money, image, and fame reported less self-actualization and vitality, and more depression than those less concerned with these values. What is more, they also reported significantly more experiences of physical symptoms. That is, people who believed it is important to strive for possessions, popularity, and good looks also reported more headaches, backaches, sore muscles, and sore throats than individuals less focused on such goals. This was really one of the first indicators, to us, of the pervasive negative correlates of materialistic values—not only is people's psychological well-being worse when they focus on money, but so is their physical health.

As in our studies of college students, materialistic values were equally unhealthy for men and women. Because of the nature of this sample, we could also examine whether findings depended on age or income. Analyses showed that regardless of their age or wealth, people with highly central materialistic values also reported lower well-being.

Having documented some of the problems associated with materialism in adults of different ages and backgrounds, we returned to college students and teenagers to explore further the many different ways that these values are associated with low well-being. As a start, we wanted a better sense of the daily lives of people with a strong materialistic orientation. The earlier studies asked individuals to look back on some portion of their lives and tell us about their well-being; although this is a quick method to measure how people are feeling, we wanted to change the focus and obtain a snapshot of people's daily lives. Therefore, in addition to completing our standard packet of questionnaires, we asked 192 students at the University of Rochester to keep a diary for two weeks. In the middle of each day, and then again at the end of each day, they answered several questions about their current experience: how much they had the same nine physical symptoms assessed in the adult sample and how much they felt each of nine emotions (e.g., happy, joyful, unhappy, angry).

As before, participants highly focused on materialistic values reported less self-actualization and vitality and more depression than those with less interest in those values. They also experienced more physical symptoms and less in the way of positive emotions over the two weeks. Something about a strong desire for materialistic pursuits actually affected the participants' day-to-day lives and decreased the quality of their daily experience.[11]

Another new element of this study was measurement of participants' narcissistic tendencies. In psychological parlance, narcissism describes people who cover an inner feeling of emptiness and questionable self-worth with a grandiose exterior that brags of self-importance. Narcissists are typically vain, expect special treatment and admiration from others, and can be manipulative and hostile toward others. Social critics and psychologists have often suggested that consumer culture breeds a narcissistic personality by focusing individuals on the glorification of consumption (e.g., "Have it your way"; "Want it? Get it!").[12] Furthermore, narcissists' desire for external validation fits well with our conception of materialistic values as extrinsic and focused on others' praise. Thus it was not surprising to find that students with strong materialistic tendencies scored high on a standard measure of narcissism, agreeing with statements such as, "I am more capable than other people," "I like to start new fads and fashions," "I wish somebody would write my biography one day," and "I can make anybody believe anything I want them to."[13]

More recent studies expanded our measurements of psychological functioning by examining the extent to which materialism is associated with the use of substances such as tobacco, alcohol, and drugs. In one such project, Ryan and I asked 261 students at Montana State University how many cigarettes they smoked on a typical day, and how often in the last year they had "gotten drunk," "smoked marijuana," and "done hard drugs." When we averaged these four indicators, results showed that people with a strong materialistic value orientation were highly likely to use such substances frequently.[14]

These results were replicated by Geoff Williams in two groups of high school students.[15] In one study, 141 high school students were asked whether they had smoked 100 cigarettes in their lifetime, which is the National Cancer Institute's definition of a smoker. Student smokers were more oriented toward materialistic values than toward values such as self-acceptance, affiliation, and community feeling. Williams next asked

271 ninth- through twelfth-graders about an even broader list of behaviors that put teens at risk for later problems, such as use of cigarettes, chewing tobacco, alcohol, and marijuana, as well as whether they ever had sexual intercourse. Materialistic teens were more likely to engage in each of these five risk behaviors than were teens focused on other values.

Another Way to Look at Materialism

Each of the studies reviewed used the Aspiration Index as the primary means of assessing participants' materialistic values. Although the index has worked well, it also has an important limit common to all questionnaires of its type. Study participants were presented with preselected goals and aspirations that Ryan and I constructed, leaving them little room to present their own goals in the particular ways they might want to express them.

To assess materialism more on participants' own terms, Ken Sheldon and I developed a method that asks participants to begin by listing their personal goals in their own words.[16] After doing this, they are asked to think about how much each goal might help them reach different "possible futures." Participants are given a list of six futures that might occur, three of which are materialistic (financial success, fame and popularity, physical attractiveness) and three of which are not (self-acceptance and personal growth, intimacy and friendship, societal contribution). They then rate how helpful each of their goals is in reaching each of these futures. For example, a goal such as "lose 10 pounds" might help bring about the possible future of physical attractiveness, but it is unlikely to contribute much to society. People's materialistic value orientation is thus measured by the extent to which their expressed personal goals are highly oriented toward attaining possessions, attractiveness, and popularity.

This personal goal methodology has been applied to almost 500 individuals, and has successfully replicated and extended our previous findings. For example, college students focused on materialistic strivings reported low self-actualization and infrequent experiences of positive emotions.[17] In a more recent study involving 108 adults ranging in age from eighteen to seventy-two, those highly oriented toward materialistic goals also reported fewer experiences of positive emotions and less overall satisfaction with their lives than did those with less materialistic goals. As with previous work, the negative relationship between materialistic value orientations and well-being held for people of all ages and for both genders.[18]

Summary

The first chapter ended with the question, "What happens to the quality of our lives when we value materialism?" The answer, as we have seen from the studies described, is, "The more materialistic values are at the center of our lives, the more our quality of life is diminished." In samples of adolescents, college students, and adults, with various means of measuring materialistic values and well-being, results show a clear pattern of psychological (and physical) difficulties associated with holding wealth, popularity, and image as relatively important.

Other Investigators, Same Findings

My confidence that materialistic values are associated with relatively low well-being and psychological health is bolstered by the fact that other investigators have reported parallel results. For example, using the Aspiration Index or similar scales, four groups of investigators replicated our results in college students, business students, and entrepreneurs. Specifically, these studies showed that materialistic values are associated with low self-actualization and well-being, as well as more antisocial behavior and narcissism.[19]

The Research of the Cohens

Patricia and Jacob Cohen conducted a large-scale investigation yielding similar results.[20] They studied a diverse group of over 700 twelve- to twenty-year-olds living in upstate New York, and measured materialistic values in two ways. First, participants were asked how much they admired twenty-two different abilities, including getting good grades, writing stories, leading a gang, and so on. The Cohens found several groups of values that emerged from analyses of these characteristics, one of which they called materialistic. This cluster of values included the admiration of three characteristics: "having expensive possessions," "wearing expensive clothes," and "being pretty or handsome." Thus, adolescents who tended to admire one of these characteristics also tended to admire the other two. (Note the similarity to the cluster of values called extrinsic.) A second value survey assessed how much adolescents cared about twenty-one "life priorities," such as "to be a really good person," "to understand myself," and "to do what God wants me to." Most interesting for this discussion, the survey also assessed the life priority "to be rich."

The adolescents and their mothers were interviewed by psychologists using standard interviews designed to determine whether the adolescents met criteria for different disorders specified by the American Psychiatric Association in the *Diagnostic and Statistical Manual of Mental Disorders* (version 3, revised).[21] The DSM III-R, as it is called, was the standard reference used in North America to define and diagnose mental disorders at the time of this research. Adolescents were assessed for almost every important disorder mental health professionals are likely to treat, including depression, anxiety, attention deficit disorder, and behavior disorders, as well as more long-standing personality disorders such as narcissism, obsessive behavior, and paranoia (table 2.3).

To examine whether admiration of materialistic values and the priority put on being rich were associated with these disorders, the Cohens computed odds ratios. Odds ratios indicate how much more likely a highly materialistic individual is to have a disorder than someone who is not as materialistic or does not place a high priority on being rich. For example, an odds ratio of 1.00 means that teens who place a high priority on materialism are no more likely to have a particular disorder than the average person; an odds ratio of 1.50 means that materialistic teens are one and a half times as likely to have the diagnosis, and so on.

Table 2.3 reports the odds that adolescents who admired materialistic values and put a priority on being rich were diagnosed with the different disorders. For example, those who admired materialism were 1.51 times more likely to have separation anxiety disorder than adolescents who did not admire such pursuits, and those who put a priority on being rich were 1.68 times more likely to have separation anxiety disorder. As can be seen in the table, many different types of problems were characteristic of adolescents focused on materialistic pursuits.

Table 2.3

Synopses of mental disorders studied by the Cohens, and the odds ratios that adolescents who admired materialistic values or put a priority on being rich had each disorder

Disorder and description	Odds ratios	
	Materialism	Being rich
Conduct disorder—violation of rights of others or laws of society	1.14	1.29
Oppositional/defiant disorder—pattern of hostile, defiant, and disobediant behavior toward authorities	1.06	1.37
Attention deficit disorder—problems attending/concentrating, and/or hyperactivity	1.37	1.53
Alcohol abuse—pattern of alcohol use that leads to social or interpersonal problems	——	1.35
Marijuana abuse—pattern of marijuana use that leads to social or interpersonal problems	——	1.79
Separation anxiety—excessive anxiety about being separated from one's home or parents	1.51	1.68
Major depression—period of at least two weeks involving depressed or irritable mood or loss of interest in nearly all activities	——	1.22
Schizoid—lack of desire for interpersonal relationships, and lack of emotional expression	——	1.46
Schizotypal—difficulty having close relationships, combined with unusual, odd beliefs	——	2.26
Paranoid—pervasive distrust of others, shown in a belief that others are out to hurt the individual	1.60	1.43
Histrionic—excessively emotional and attention-seeking behavior	1.60	1.14
Borderline—pattern of unstable relationships, mood swings, feelings of emptiness, and self-destructive behavior	1.48	1.33
Narcissistic—grandiosity, seeking excessive admiration from others, but lacking empathy	1.52	1.40
Passive-aggressive—opposing demands through passive means, such as procrastinating or being intentionally inefficient	1.49	2.23
Dependent—excessive need to be taken care of, expressed by submissive and clinging behavior	1.80	1.34

Table 2.3
(continued)

	Odds ratios	
Disorder and description	Materialism	Being rich
Avoidant—strong concern with the negative evaluations of others, leading to avoidance of social interactions	——	1.59
Obsessive-compulsive—being preoccupied with orderliness and control, at the expense of flexibility and openness	——	1.18

Dashes indicate no significant effect.
Modified from Cohen and Cohen, 1995; reprinted by permission of Lawrence Erlbaum.

Not only do these results confirm many of the findings reported in our lab, they also substantially expand the list of problems associated with materialistic values. Specifically, compared to nonmaterialistic teens, those with a strong orientation to materialistic values are also more likely to have difficulties with attention, exhibit unusual thoughts and behaviors, isolate themselves socially, believe others have malevolent intentions, have difficulties with emotional expression and controlling impulses, be either avoidant or overly dependent on other people, attempt to overcontrol many aspects of their environment, and relate to people in a passive-aggressive manner.

The Cohens summarized the breadth of these problems by concluding, "The priority put on being rich was related positively to almost every . . . diagnosis assessed in this study, for the most part significantly so."[22]

Consumer Research

Another set of studies investigating relationships between materialism and well-being comes from the disciplines of marketing and consumer research. I must admit that I was at first surprised to discover a body of literature on the problems of materialism in a field that attempts to understand how to market products and convince individuals to consume them. As I worked to overcome my stereotypes, however, I found that this literature is full of insights about the effects of materialism on people.

The earliest data demonstrating a negative relationship between materialism and well-being were presented by Russell Belk in two papers, in 1984 and 1985.[23] As can be seen in table 2.4, Belk measured a materialistic outlook by assessing three main characteristics or traits. First, materialistic people are *possessive,* in that they prefer to own and keep things rather than borrow, rent, or throw things out. Second, materialistic individuals are *nongenerous,* or unwilling to share their possessions with others. Third, materialistic people tend to *envy* the possessions of others, feeling displeasure when others have things they themselves desire.

The materialism survey was administered to a sample of over 300 individuals, including business students, machine shop workers, students at a religious institute, and secretaries at an insurance office. Participants were also asked two questions about well-being: "How happy are you?" and "How satisfied are you with your life?" Compared with people low in materialism, those who were possessive, nongenerous, and envious of others' possessions were likely to report that they were less happy and less satisfied with their lives. Since Belk's initial study, three other papers replicated these findings, and other studies demonstrated that materialism is associated with depression and social anxiety.[24]

Another important consumer research study was performed by marketing professors Marsha Richins and Scott Dawson.[25] These investigators developed a scale that assesses how much people think possessions reflect success in life, how central materialism is to their desires, and how much they believe wealth and possessions yield happiness (table 2.5). This conceptualization of materialism includes not only the desire to make money and have possessions, but also the desire to own things that impress others and that elicit some sense of social recognition. It thus contains items tapping some of the related values (for image and popularity) that studies cited above found cluster together.

Eight hundred randomly selected individuals (primarily adults living in the northeastern and western United States) participated in this study. In addition to completing this measure of materialism, participants were asked how satisfied they were generally with their lives as well as in specific areas, such as family, job, and so on. Compared with nonmaterialistic respondents, those with a strong materialistic orientation reported less

Table 2.4
Items from Belk's (1985) materialism scale

Possessiveness
Renting or leasing a car is more appealing to me than owning one.*
I tend to hang on to things I should probably throw out.
I get very upset if something is stolen from me, even if it has little monetary value.
I don't get particularly upset when I lose things.*
I am less likely than most people to lock things up.*
I would rather buy something I need than borrow it from someone else.
I worry about people taking my possessions.
When I travel I like to take a lot of photographs.
I never discard old pictures or snapshots.

Nongenerosity
I enjoy having guests stay in my home.*
I enjoy sharing what I have.*
I don't like to lend things, even to good friends.
It makes sense to buy a lawnmower with a neighbor and share it.*
I don't mind giving rides to those who don't have a car.*
I don't like to have anyone in my home when I'm not there.
I enjoy donating things to charity.*

Envy
I am bothered when I see people who buy anything they want.
I don't know anyone whose spouse or steady date I would like to have as my own.*
When friends do better than me in competition it usually makes me happy for them.*
People who are very wealthy often feel they are too good to talk to average people.
There are certain people I would like to trade places with.
When friends have things I cannot afford it bothers me.
I don't seem to get what is coming to me.
When Hollywood stars or prominent politicians have things stolen from them I really feel sorry for them.*

Participants are asked how strongly they agree or disagree with these statements.
Items with a * are scored so that disagreement indicates higher materialism.
Reprinted by permission of the University of Chicago Press.

Table 2.5
Sample items from Richins and Dawson's (1992) materialism scale

---

Success
I admire people who own expensive homes, cars, and clothes.
Some of the most important achievements in life include acquiring material possessions.
I don't place much emphasis on the amount of material objects a person owns as a sign of success.*
The things I own say a lot about how well I'm doing in life.
I like to own things that impress people.
I don't pay much attention to the material objects other people own.*

Centrality
I usually buy only the things I need.*
I try to keep my life simple, as far as possessions are concerned.*
The things I own aren't all that important to me.*
I enjoy spending money on things that aren't practical.
Buying things gives me a lot of pleasure.
I like a lot of luxury in my life.
I put less emphasis on material things than most people I know.*

Happiness
I have all the things I really need to enjoy life.*
My life would be better if I owned certain things I don't have.
I wouldn't be any happier if I owned nicer things.*
I'd be happier if I could afford to buy more things.
It sometimes bothers me quite a bit that I can't afford to buy all the things I'd like.

Participants are presented with these statements and asked how strongly they agree or disagree with them. Items with a * are scored so that disagreement indicates more materialism.
Reprinted by permission of the University of Chicago Press.

satisfaction with their lives overall, with their family, their income, and their relationships with friends, as well as with how much fun they have. Other authors using Richins and Dawson's questionnaire have since found that materialistic people reported lower life satisfaction and self-actualization than nonmaterialistic people.[26]

In summary, other investigators studying materialism have reached essentially the same conclusion as I have: materialistic values are associated with low well-being.

Other Cultures, Same Findings

All of the studies reviewed thus far were conducted in the United States. It is interesting to know that one of the world's wealthiest, most powerful nations appears to be inculcating values not conducive to its citizens' well-being, but the possibility remains that the results are specific to the United States. Perhaps this phenomenon is the result of certain cultural features, such as the economy, television shows, or history, and does not hold in other cultures.

To address this issue, several studies have used translated versions of the Aspiration Index and of personal well-being measures in samples of people from around the world. Thus far, studies with British, Danish, German, Indian, Romanian, Russian, and South Korean college students have confirmed the negative associations between materialistic values and well-being. These findings were replicated with German adults, and similar results were found in business students from Singapore.[27]

Other investigators have also reported similar results in other countries. For example, Shaun Saunders and Don Munro found that a materialistic outlook in Australian students was associated with increased feelings of anger, anxiety, and depression, and with decreased life satisfaction. Another study headed by Joe Sirgy showed that life satisfaction was diminished when adults in China, Turkey, Australia, Canada, and the United States scored as highly materialistic on either the Belk or Richins and Dawson's scales; similar results have been reported in samples of adults in Singapore. Finally, Edward Diener and Shige Oishi collected value and life satisfaction measures from over 7,000 college students in 41 different nations. Again, a strong value on making money was associated with diminishing life satisfaction.[28]

Thus, findings from samples of individuals all over the world show that a strong relative focus on materialistic values is associated with low well-being. In some countries the results are fairly strong, and although they are somewhat weaker in others, the general pattern is consistent. What is more, results do not support the idea that placing strong importance on materialistic values is associated with greater well-being.[29] This is important, as some theoretical perspectives might suggest that people in developing capitalist economies such as Russia or India, or countries such as Singapore where shopping is a highly encouraged national pastime, could increase their well-being when they internalize the pervasive consumer messages their cultures propound. Once again, the opposite is the case: materialistic values appear not to bring happiness and well-being, but instead more anxiety, little vitality, few pleasant emotions, and low life satisfaction.

Summary

Existing scientific research on the value of materialism yields clear and consistent findings. People who are highly focused on materialistic values have lower personal well-being and psychological health than those who believe that materialistic pursuits are relatively unimportant. These relationships have been documented in samples of people ranging from the wealthy to the poor, from teenagers to the elderly, and from Australians to South Koreans. Several investigators have reported similar results using a variety of ways of measuring materialism. The studies document that strong materialistic values are associated with a pervasive undermining of people's well-being, from low life satisfaction and happiness, to depression and anxiety, to physical problems such as headaches, and to personality disorders, narcissism, and antisocial behavior.

Not the picture of psychological health painted by the commercials, is it?

3

Psychological Needs

But Mom, I *need* that toy.
—Anonymous child

The evidence just presented documents that when people are strongly oriented to materialistic values they also experience low well-being. But why is this true? Do materialistic values cause people's problems? If so, how? Or is it the case that people who are already unhappy focus on wealth, possessions, image, and popularity? If so, why?

The answers to these questions are clearly complicated, and the scientists' mantra, "More research is needed," has rarely been more pertinent. Yet I believe that a sound theory can be constructed to explain much of what researchers have found concerning materialism's "dark side." The theory that my colleagues and I have been developing is based in the idea of psychological needs, and it is with this concept that we must begin.

Psychological Needs

The idea that people have psychological needs is both popular and controversial. Although no one disagrees that all people have certain physical needs (e.g., air, water, and food) that must be met to ensure survival, some social scientists stop there, saying that psychological needs are either impossible to prove scientifically or do not exist. Yet other theorists and researchers apply the concept of psychological needs to understand human motivation and well-being,[1] and even those who eschew the concept per se talk as though certain psychological processes are basic to human motivation and must operate in particular ways for people to function optimally.[2]

What then is a need?[3] A need, in the sense used here, is not just something a person desires or wants, but is something that is necessary to his or her survival, growth, and optimal functioning. Just as a plant must have air, water, light, and a certain soil chemistry to survive and thrive, all people require certain "psychological nutriments" for their health and growth. Furthermore, just as a plant turns toward light and reaches its roots down to find water and minerals, needs direct us to behave in ways that increase the likelihood that they will be satisfied. Thus needs motivate behavior and require fulfillment for psychological growth to occur.

Even if we agree that needs motivate the basic experiences and behaviors necessary for survival and optimal functioning, students of the human situation still argue about the number of needs we have and about what to call them. On the basis of psychological research and theorizing, I have come to conclude that at least four sets of needs are basic to the motivation, functioning, and well-being of all humans. Described in more detail below, I call them needs for safety, security, and sustenance; for competence, efficacy, and self-esteem; for connectedness; and for autonomy and authenticity.[4] Each set of needs has been described by theorists from various psychological perspectives, and each has been empirically associated with humans' quality of life. In addition, as we will see in later chapters, each of these needs appears to be relatively unfulfilled when people hold materialistic pursuits as central in their value systems.

Let us first consider the needs for safety, security, and sustenance. These are the needs we have for food on our tables, a roof over our heads, and clothing to protect us from the weather—the essentials of life. They also reflect the fact that we do not function well when constantly exposed to harmful, anxiety-provoking, and unstable situations. When we are young, these needs often manifest themselves in our desire to know that our parents will care for us and help us survive and thrive. Security needs basically represent our desire to remain alive and avoid what might lead to early death.[5]

The second set of needs involves a feeling that we are capable of doing what we set out to do and of obtaining the things we value. Competence and esteem needs also entail a desire to have a more positive than negative view of ourselves and to like ourselves. In essence, to fulfill these needs each of us must feel like a competent and worthy person.[6]

The third set of needs is for being connected and related to other people. Humans strongly desire intimacy and closeness with others, going to great lengths to seek out and secure such relationships. These needs lead us to belong to larger groups, such as churches, neighborhood organizations, and teams. We need to feel that we belong and are connected with others' lives, be it as parents, friends, neighbors, or coworkers.[7]

Finally, we need to feel autonomous and authentically engaged in our behavior. We constantly strive for increased freedom and more opportunities to experience life in a self-directed manner. These needs are most apparent in our strong motivation to express ourselves and to follow our own personal interests. Rather than feeling pressured or burdened by our circumstances, we need to pursue activities that provide us with challenge, interest, and enjoyment. By doing so, we can feel ownership of our own behavior, and thus feel both authentic and autonomous.[8]

To summarize, substantial research and theory suggest that people are highly motivated to feel safe and secure, competent, connected to others, and autonomous and authentically engaged in their behavior. This literature proposes that well-being and quality of life increase when these four sets of needs are satisfied and decrease when they are not.

Need Expression and Satisfaction

Although needs provide a basic motivation to do something, they do not tell us exactly how to satisfy them. The way needs express themselves and the extent to which they are satisfied depend on a number of factors, including our personality, lifestyle, values, and the culture in which we live.

For example, if I am hungry, my need for sustenance motivates me to eat. The way that I satisfy this need will vary depending on my personal tastes and on my environment. If I like sweet foods, I might seek out an orange or some candy; if I like salty foods, I might prefer pretzels or potato chips; if I live in Japan, I might eat sushi; if I live in Lebanon, I will be likely to eat hummus. Personality and societal context provide frameworks for need expression and satisfaction by suggesting particular pathways and behaviors we might follow. In many cases, these frameworks do a reasonably good job of satisfying our needs, and thus of supporting psychological health and well-being.

Consider what would happen, however, if every time I was hungry I ate chocolate cake; many of my body's physical needs for certain nutrients would remain unfulfilled, and my health would surely suffer. In a similar manner, it is not necessarily the case that our personalities and culture provide healthy pathways that adequately satisfy psychological needs. Instead, aspects of our personalities and life circumstances sometimes lead us to try to satisfy our needs in ways that are ultimately unfulfilling. And sometimes our environments fail to furnish many opportunities for healthy expression of our needs, and thus lead us astray from the ways of life that could really help us to be happy.

When we look around at contemporary consumer culture it is clear that people are constantly bombarded with messages that needs can be satisfied by having the right products. Feel unsafe on the road or in your home? Buy the right tire or lock. Worried that you will die young? Eat this cereal and take out insurance from that company just in case. Lawn look bad in comparison with your neighbor's? Buy this lawnmower and fertilizer. Can't get a date? Buy these clothes, this shampoo, and that deodorant. No adventure in your life? Take this vacation, buy that sport utility vehicle, or subscribe to these magazines. Consumer societies also provide many role models suggesting that a high quality of life (i.e., need satisfaction) occurs when one has successfully attained material goals. Heroes and heroines of consumeristic cultures are on the whole wealthy, good-looking, and often famous. These are the people, we are told, who are successful, whose lives we should strive to imitate and emulate.

In the face of messages glorifying the path of consumption and wealth, all of us to some extent take on or internalize materialistic values. That is, we incorporate the messages of consumer society into our own value and belief systems. These values then begin to organize our lives by influencing the goals we pursue, the attitudes we have toward particular people and objects, and the behaviors in which we engage.[9]

Almost all of us place at least some importance on possessions, money, and image, but materialism takes hold of the center of some people's value systems. As a consequence, their experiences will be changed. To illustrate, take two people, one who values material wealth more than helping others, and another with the opposite set of priorities. When confronted with a decision about what career to pursue, the materialistic individual will be likely to seek out a high-paying, high-status job with many opportunities to earn a great deal of money. In contrast, the less materialistic individual will be likely to accept a lower-paying job if it will benefit others. Or imagine that both individuals are presented with a special issue of *Forbes* magazine about how wealthy people obtained their riches. The materialistic person will likely read the magazine with interest, while the other individual will likely become quickly bored. What these examples show is that the two people's lives, and thus the experiences they have, are quite different as a result of their values.

The different experiences of these two individuals will influence the extent to which their needs are ultimately satisfied. Just as a person who eats junk food will be less healthy than one who eats many fruits and vegetables, an individual with relatively central materialistic values will have fewer chances to fulfill the needs required for psychological growth and happiness. As we will see in chapters to come, materialistic values lead people into a style of life and way of experiencing that do a rather poor job of satisfying their needs. Taking our nutritional metaphor a bit farther, consumer society sells junk food, promising that it tastes good and makes us happy. As a result, many people buy it. Alas, they are full for only a short time, as the promise is false and the satisfaction is empty.

Individual Differences in Internalization

Given that most of us are exposed to similar cultural messages encouraging materialism, why is it that some of us internalize these values more than others? Why did the first individual in the example above care more about wealth and possessions than the second person? One explanation involves the extent to which people have been exposed to the messages of consumer culture. For example, people are likely to be materialistic if they watch a great deal of television and if their parents value materialistic goals.[10] So part of the answer is that some people simply learn this attitude or outlook because of their environment.

But it is also the case that people's preexisting level of need satisfaction causes them to value certain outcomes differently.[11] As Abraham Maslow wrote, when people have a particular need that is not well satisfied, their "whole philosophy of the future tends also to change. For our chronically and extremely hungry man, Utopia can be defined simply as a place where there is plenty of food. He tends to think that, if only he is guaranteed food for the rest of his life, he will be perfectly happy and will never want anything more."[12] The same dynamic seems to occur in the case of materialism. Individuals who have not had their needs well met in the past come to think that wealth and possessions will bring them happiness and a good life. Part of this belief is due to the fact that society tells them the material path will make them feel secure, and part is because our bodies require some material comforts to survive. In any case, a strong focus on materialistic values is often a symptom or manifestation of a personal history characterized by a relative failure in need satisfaction. These unmet needs thus lead people to be unhappy and to develop materialistic values.

Summary

In this chapter I proposed that people have needs that must be satisfied for them to have a high quality of life. Materialistic values become prominent in the lives of some individuals who have a history of not having their needs well met. Thus, one reason these values are associated with a low quality of life is that they are symptoms or signs that some needs remain unfulfilled. But materialistic values are not just expressions of unhappiness. Instead, they lead people to organize their lives in ways that do a poor job of satisfying their needs, and thus contribute even more to people's misery.

The next four chapters review scientific evidence supporting these ideas. As shown in chapter 4, materialistic values become prominent when people's needs for safety and sustenance are inadequately satisfied. Chapter 5 reveals that needs for esteem and competence suffer due to several dynamics associated with materialistic pursuits. Chapters 6 and 7 demonstrate that such values interfere with achieving high-quality relationships and feelings of freedom and authenticity in life. The literature reviewed in these chapters thus not only supports the theory my colleagues and I developed, but extends evidence showing that materialistic pursuits fail to bring about an optimally meaningful and high-quality life.

4

Insecurity

But the fear of death grew ever darker upon them, and . . . those that lived turned the more eagerly to pleasure and revelry, desiring ever more goods and more riches.

—J. R. R. Tolkien[1]

Tolkien's epic myth of humanity's origin recognizes a fundamental truth: when sustenance and survival are threatened, people search for material resources to help them feel safe and secure. Just as our ancestors had to collect berries to fill their baskets, hunt woolly mammoths with their spears, and build shelter with available materials, contemporary humans must earn a paycheck and pay the bills. Having a steady job and money in a savings account make people feel more secure and thus fulfill the same needs that drove our ancestors to store dried meat for another long winter. There is no doubt that humans require some material necessities and comforts in order to feel secure and stay alive.

Although all people seek material means of meeting their sustenance, safety, and security needs, some focus on materialistic pursuits to a much greater extent. Let's face it: a $60,000 Mercedes is not necessary for survival. But even though such luxury goods seem far beyond what is required to live, a number of psychologists and social scientists suggest that people who highly value materialistic aims are driven by unmet needs for security and safety.[2] From this perspective, materialistic values are both a symptom of underlying insecurity and a coping strategy (albeit a relatively ineffective one) some people use in an attempt to alleviate their anxieties.

This chapter illustrates the associations between materialistic values and insecurity by presenting several types of evidence. First, I review studies demonstrating that individuals orient toward materialistic values when they have experienced family circumstances that do not help them feel secure. Second, I show that broader cultural conditions that undermine feelings of security also produce a strong focus on materialistic values. Finally, I discuss research that has probed into the psyches of materialistic people and revealed processes associated with insecurity that generally occur outside of conscious awareness.

Materialism and the Family

The family is of course the primary socializing environment for most of our early years, and the experiences we have there strongly determine how much we eventually feel safe and secure. The ways parents treat their children, the stability of the family, and the socioeconomic circumstances in which children are raised each have important ramifications in terms of fulfilling needs for safety, sustenance, and security. As detailed below, when family environments poorly satisfy needs for security, many children respond by adopting a value system that emphasizes wealth and possessions.

Parental Styles and Materialism

Parental practices have been recognized for decades as playing an extremely important role in children's lives. Literally thousands of studies have explored how characteristics of parental styles, such as warmth and control, influence various aspects of children's personality and social-emotional development. Recently some of these same factors were investigated in relationship to materialistic values.

Richard Ryan, Melvin Zax, Arnold Sameroff, and I explored this issue in the heterogeneous group of 140 eighteen-year-olds described in chapter 2.[3] In addition to collecting information about teenagers' aspirations and personal adjustment, we interviewed their mothers to find out how the young people were being raised. Our primary purpose was to measure how nurturant the mothers were with their children, that is, how much they supported their children's security versus how much they did not.

Trained interviewers talked for an hour with each mother and rated the emotions she expressed about her child. Some mothers spoke with warmth, pride, and enjoyment about the child ("Jane is such a good girl, she always helps out around the house"), and others were more likely to reveal disapproval, criticism, or hostility toward their child ("That Johnny is a real pain in the neck and is just plain lazy"). Mothers also completed a sixty-eight-item survey about their parenting philosophies. From this, we obtained measures of their tendency to be warm, affectionate, and appreciative of their children, whether they imposed many rules and strictures on their children, and how much they allowed their children to express their own opinions and to be their own person.[4]

These five variables (three from the survey and two from the interview) were combined into a measure of maternal nurturance. Our assumption was that a less-nurturing parenting style would lead children to feel rather insecure about their worth as people and thus to express more materialistic values. As predicted, when teenagers who strongly valued financial success were compared with those who placed more value on self-acceptance, good relationships, or contributing to the community, the materialistic teens had mothers who were less nurturing.

Two studies have replicated and extended these results.[5] In one, Geoff Williams found that materialistic teenagers perceived their parents as relatively unlikely to listen to their perspectives, acknowledge their feelings, or provide them with choices. In the second study, Patricia and Jacob Cohen showed that teenagers highly oriented toward materialistic values had parents with three principal characteristics. First, the parents were highly enmeshed with or possessive of their children, believing that their children could not really take care of themselves alone. Second, they were likely to use harsh, punitive measures when their children misbehaved. Finally, they were unlikely to provide much structure for their children, being lax in the consistency with which they applied certain rules to their children's behavior. All three of these parental practices are unlikely to meet children's needs for security and safety.

Such findings thus suggest that materialistic teenagers may be raised by parents who do not do as much as they might to help their children feel secure, valued as people, and safe. The resultant feelings of insecurity are then expressed (in part) by a strong tendency to focus on materialistic pursuits. I believe there are several reasons for this type of compensation, although more research is required to support my speculations. First, children who experience nonnurturant parenting may be especially susceptible to consumer messages that prey on our insecurities and promise happiness and security through consumption. Second, children who feel insecure about themselves may be likely to look for approval from other people in order to feel better about themselves. Because they are exposed to frequent messages in society glorifying image, fame, and wealth, they may strongly pursue materialistic aspirations as a way to obtain that approval.

Divorce

Research shows that divorce is also related to a focus on materialistic values. Aric Rindfleisch and his colleagues surveyed 261 young adults ranging in age between twenty and thirty-two, from a medium-size Midwestern city.[6] When the 165 participants from nondivorced families were compared with the 96 from divorced families, the latter were more likely to be materialistic (as measured by the Richins and Dawson scale).

Rindfleisch and his colleagues also explored whether these effects of divorce on materialistic values were due primarily to the financial strain of divorce. On the basis of further statistical analysis, they concluded, "it is the diminution of interpersonal resources such as love and affection, rather than financial resources, that links family disruption and materialism."[7] In other words, when families experience divorce, parents' ability to engage in optimal parenting practices often diminishes, leading children to experience lessened warmth and nurturance. As a result, many children turn to materialistic pursuits as a way of trying to fill this gap and feel more safe, secure, and connected to others. This strategy does not appear to be very effective, as we will see.

Family Socioeconomic Status

On the face of it, the third family characteristic known to produce materialistic children is rather counterintuitive. Many people assume that greater wealth is associated with greater materialism, as children from rich families seem to have most everything they could possibly desire and often want even more. Yet data on materialistic values are more consistent with the thesis developed here: poverty creates circumstances in which people worry about satisfying their basic sustenance and security needs, and in an attempt to fulfill these needs, a significant number of them become oriented to materialistic goals. Growing up unsure of where one's next meal will come from, how long one will be in the current apartment, and whether one is safe stepping outside the door can all lead to chronic feelings of insecurity. These feelings can often last throughout one's life, even if one's economic circumstances improve, and may eventually be manifest in materialistic tendencies.

In the work my colleagues and I conducted with the heterogeneous sample of teens previously described, we collected information on the education and occupations of the parents, and also obtained United States Census and police record information about the average income and crime rates in the neighborhood in which the teen was living at the time of the interview. Teenagers who strongly valued materialism were more likely to come from poorer backgrounds than were children who valued self-acceptance, relationships, and community contribution.[8] Similarly, the Cohens reported that children from families of low socioeconomic backgrounds also admired materialistic values more and placed a higher priority on "being rich." Although little direct effect of neighborhoods on materialistic values was seen in their study, materialistic children attended schools in which teachers were unable to maintain order, and where students were likely to defy authority, fight, and vandalize.[9] Obviously, such academic settings are unlikely to lead children to feel very safe.

These findings suggest that growing up in poverty and poor neighborhoods may be partly responsible for creating a materialistic value orientation. I believe this association is due to the fact that such social environments often lead children to feel unsafe and insecure, and these unmet needs drive them to value the materialistic pursuits encouraged by society.

Materialism and the Nation

The family is only one environment to which we are exposed, and one source of experience that may or may not fulfill our security needs. We also exist in communities, cultures, and nations, and the circumstances inherent in these socializing units influence need satisfaction and thus the values we adopt. As is the case with families, when cultural circumstances fail to support and satisfy needs for security, safety, and sustenance, evidence shows that people are increasingly likely to value materialistic pursuits.

The Cross-Cultural Work of Ronald Inglehart

For the last three decades, political scientist Ronald Inglehart has been exploring the causes and ramifications of people's focus on materialistic values.[10] To this end, he and his colleagues have been conducting research around the world contrasting materialistic and what he calls "post-materialistic" value orientations. Unlike investigators discussed thus far, Inglehart is more interested in social than in personal values. That is, all of the scales described so far ask people how much they value wealth for themselves. In contrast, Inglehart assesses materialism by asking what people think should be the aims of their society and government.

Inglehart asks individuals to examine a number of different values and to choose the ones most important to them. Some of the values are primarily concerned with maintaining a strong economy, national security, and social stability. These are considered to be materialistic values. Post-materialistic values, in contrast, involve freedom, environmental beauty, and civility. Inglehart believes that materialistic values primarily derive from unmet needs for safety and sustenance, whereas postmaterialistic values reflect higher-level needs for esteem, belongingness, knowledge, and aesthetics.[10]

A central thesis in this work is that national occurrences that threaten needs for safety and security lead people to focus on materialistic values at the expense of postmaterialistic values. To test this idea, Inglehart has surveyed tens of thousands of people around the world. Although he has tested a large number of ideas with this body of data, three basic findings concern us here.[11]

First, data consistently show that older individuals are more materialistic than younger individuals. One study demonstrating this effect was conducted with over 200,000 people living in West Germany, France, Britain, Italy, The Netherlands and Belgium. Inglehart's explanation for why older people are more materialistic is not developmental, but is based on historical causes. The theory is that because contemporary older people were generally raised in times of great economic scarcity and world upheaval (the Great Depression, World War II), their needs for safety and security were less well met than were the needs of people born in the last decades of the twentieth century, who have lived in relative economic prosperity and peace.[12] Thus, contemporary younger people focus on postmaterialistic goals because their needs for sustenance and safety were consistently met when they were children. Inglehart's predictions suggest that younger people could become more materialistic if the world were struck by another wave of economic hard times or widespread war. Let us hope that this hypothesis remains untested.

The second important point of Inglehart's research (for our purposes) concerns fluctuations in levels of materialism and postmaterialism. Although individuals remain fairly consistent in their values as they age, at certain times people of all ages become more materialistic. For example, short-term changes toward increased materialism corresponded with western European recessions in the mid-1970s, early 1980s, and early 1990s, and seemed to be primarily a function of national inflation rates. This shows that people become more materialistic during economically harder, and thus less secure, times.

These results raise a third question: what about the materialism of rich and poor nations? To examine this, Inglehart and colleagues conducted the 1990–1991 world values survey, which surveyed almost 50,000 people from 40 societies around the world. Parallel to results concerning family socioeconomic status, people in poorer nations, who presumably experienced more insecurity, were typically more materialistic than those in wealthier nations.

To summarize this research, substantial evidence from a variety of cultures indicates that people especially value materialism when they belong to older cohorts of western Europeans who experienced substantial economic and national insecurity in their youth; are surveyed during periods of high economic inflation; and are citizens of poor nations that struggle with economic security. Each of these points is consistent with the hypothesis that a materialistic orientation develops when individuals have experiences (especially in childhood) that fail to support their needs for security, safety, and sustenance.

What Do Women Want in a Man?

Another approach to understanding how national characteristics influence materialistic values explored the issue reflected in the following quotation: "A woman needs four animals in her life: A mink in the closet. A jaguar in the garage. A tiger in bed. And an ass to pay for it all."[13] This comment reflects the stereotypical notion that some women desire mates who are wealthy and of high social status. As it turns out, this stereotype is rather well supported by dozens of psychological studies in cultures around the world showing that when people are asked about the characteristics they desire in a mate, women are more likely than men to express a preference for wealthy, ambitious, high-status mates.[14]

Although the dominant explanation for women's desire is that it is evolutionarily imprinted in females' nervous systems, many feminist scholars point to cultural circumstances that fail to provide women opportunities to meet their security and sustenance needs on their own.[15] Evidence supporting this perspective was scant until Yadika Sharma and I applied the logic of the position being developed here and revealed a cultural (rather than evolutionary) explanation for this gender difference.[16] Specifically, this research explored the possibility that national characteristics that might make women feel rather insecure also motivate them to become more concerned with materialistic qualities in potential mates.

We used a database collected in the mid-1980s that asked over 9,000 males and females from 37 cultures to rate how much they desired qualities in potential mates such as emotional stability, maturity, similarity in religious or educational background, and chastity.[17] We focused on three characteristics having to do with a mate's ability to provide resources: being a good financial prospect, having a favorable social status or ranking, and having the traits of ambition and industriousness.

To measure the amount of security women might experience in their respective cultures, we used data from United Nations sources about two issues especially relevant to female security. First, female reproductive freedom was assessed based on how much each culture supported women's ability to control their own reproduction and home life. For example, we examined the maternal mortality rate in each nation, whether women had access to contraceptives, and whether they were protected from domestic violence by national laws. Second, women's education equality was measured by determining the percentage of women, compared with men, who could read and write and who received primary and secondary school education.

In nations where women were provided with little opportunity to become educated (and thus fend for themselves), women expressed a stronger preference for wealthy, high-status mates than those in nations where they were educated equally to men. Similarly, women who lived in nations that did not provide much ability to control their own reproductive capacities were more interested in materialistic characteristics in mates than those who could control how many babies they might have. Notably, these results remained significant even after accounting for national wealth.

In essence, when women have less opportunity to become educated or to control their reproduction, they are likely to feel less secure about their abilities to fend for themselves, and thus are more materialistic in the desires they have for mates. These results reflect the same dynamic I discussed regarding the relationship of materialism to other forms of environmental insecurity. Across different study designs, the essential findings remain the same: materialistic values increase when environmental circumstances fail to support needs for security and safety.

Materialism and Nonconscious Processes

Thus far I have stated that nonnurturing environmental conditions induce a basic feeling of insecurity in people that is often compensated for by the pursuit of material aims. None of the studies reviewed, however, really looked "within" individuals to see whether such feelings lurk behind materialistic values and pursuits. Although we cannot always expect individuals to report their true motivations for pursuing certain goals accurately, methods exist for delving below conscious expressions to explore the experiences that may motivate them. Two recent studies used such methods to provide more support for the idea that insecurity drives people to focus on materialistic goals, even if they may not consciously admit to such motivational underpinnings.

Dreams

Although some modern researchers seem to believe that dreams are little more than random brain noise, substantial clinical and empirical work suggests that dreams often reflect many interesting facets of an individual's personality that may be somewhat inaccessible to their conscious mind. That is, dreams can reveal, in a highly symbolic way, many primary conflicts, concerns, and motivations behind people's behaviors and personalities. With these ideas in mind, my wife, Virginia Grow Kasser, and I set out to see whether they might tell us something about materialistic values as well.[18]

We studied undergraduates whose materialism scores on the Aspiration Index placed them in either the top or bottom 10 percent in comparison with their peers. We then asked these individuals to share the two most meaningful, memorable, or powerful dreams they remembered in their lives. Information collected from dreams is of course quite different from responses to surveys, and although dreams can certainly be coded and quantified into numbers, we thought it best to let them speak for themselves. Although this study is therefore less methodologically rigorous than others reviewed in this book, I nonetheless believe it is important to note that the themes discovered in quantitative research were also revealed by this more qualitative approach. To me, this is an interesting way of replicating research and showing that issues underlying a strong orientation to materialistic values can be discovered regardless of the type of study.

In looking for themes relevant to feelings of insecurity, we found three notable differences between the dreams of people high and low in materialism.

First, death played a bigger role in the dreams of highly materialistic individuals. It was mentioned in the dream itself or in associations with the dream in 20.5 percent of high materialists' dreams, compared with only 3 percent of dreams of people less focused on materialism. To give a couple of examples, people who were dead in waking life appeared in the dreams of two highly materialistic individuals, and another saw "a ghostly lady dressed in black . . . hanging from the cross [of a church] calling my name." For others who strongly valued materialistic aims, death was mentioned as an important association, even when it did not appear explicitly in the dream.

The second difference relevant to insecurity was that 15 percent of dreams of people in the high-materialism group involved falling, in comparison with 3 percent of dreams of those in the low-materialism group. Falling is almost universally interpreted by theorists as representing insecurity,[19] as one is out of control, is headed downward, and has nothing to hold on to. Two people from the high-materialism group reported dreams of falling into fires, a third fell from barn rafters, and a fourth worried about falling from logging equipment. Evocatively, a fifth person in that group dreamed that his father tossed him over the railing of the steps inside his house, but "instead of landing on the floor below, there was nothing but black space into which I was thrown . . . I saw myself fall. While I was falling into the black void, I was circling or spinning and screaming, but my screams were very faint."

Another difference between the groups was that the dreams of highly materialistic individuals exhibited a very different attitude toward feared objects. Specifically, 18 percent of dreams of the low-materialism group involved reframing an originally feared object so that it was no longer so frightening; no one from the high-materialism group confronted their fears in this way. For example, two dreamers from the low-materialism group were initially afraid of a rhinoceros and a giant purple poodle, respectively, but found that the animals had benign intentions. Others in that group realized that their attacker was actually "a nice, happy guy" or were quite confident that they would not be hurt. One of them even reported that while being chased down cliffs by a boulder, "sometimes it was rather fun to run." These dreams suggest that people who do not care much for materialistic pursuits may be more able to overcome insecurities than those with a strong materialistic value orientation.

Death

For many of us, death is insecurity par excellence, the ultimate in what is frightening. Indeed, work in social psychology suggests that our sense of self and self-esteem, as well as the phenomenon of culture as a whole, may be little more than humanity's attempts to ward off the unremitting terror associated with knowledge of one's own demise. This view, based on the writings of Ernest Becker and elaborated by Jeff Greenberg, Tom Pyszczynski, and Sheldon Solomon, is called Terror Management theory.[20] The theory has spawned dozens of studies showing that when individuals are confronted with the fact of death, they afterward are increasingly likely to denigrate those who break cultural norms, applaud those who uphold the norms, and generally mold their own behavior to gain a sense of esteem by fitting in to the spoken and unspoken rules of society. Presumably they are motivated to do these things as a way of lessening the terror aroused by thinking of their own death.

The methods of Terror Management theory struck Ken Sheldon and me as an intriguing way of experimentally activating the feelings of insecurity proposed to underlie materialistic behavior. That is, if thinking of death is terrifying, it is likely to lead to feelings of insecurity. If materialistic pursuits are an attempt to compensate for those feelings, people should become more materialistic after thinking about death. The fact that death was a prominent theme in dreams of people high in materialism made these ideas seem even more plausible.

We randomly assigned college students to either a "mortality salience" or control condition.[21] In the mortality salience condition, participants wrote short essays in response to two statements: "describe the feelings that the thought of your own death arouses in you," and "describe what you think will happen to you physically as you die and once you are dead." Participants in the control condition answered parallel questions about listening to music.

In the first study, all participants were next asked to think fifteen years in the future and to report, in today's dollars, their expectations about nine aspects of their future financial situation. From these nine ratings, we computed three sets of expectations: *overall financial worth* (expectations about their own salary and that of their spouse, worth of their home, worth of their investments, and amount they would spend on travel); *pleasure spending* (expectations about the amount they would spend on clothing, entertainment, and leisure activities); and *value of possessions* (expected worth of their vehicles and possessions in their homes).

Compared with people who wrote about listening to music, those who wrote about death reported higher expected overall financial worth in fifteen years. The same was true for the amount they expected to spend on pleasure items. For example, participants who wrote about death said they would spend an average of $813 per month on entertainment, leisure, and clothing, whereas those who wrote about music expected to spend an average of $410.

A second study approached the measurement of materialism in a somewhat different manner. After answering the essay questions about either death or music, a new group of students played a "forest-management" game. They imagined that they owned a company that was bidding against three other companies to harvest timber in a national forest. They were reminded that their company had to make a profit to survive, but that cutting large amounts of timber year after year might destroy the forest. Participants then answered three questions. First, we assessed whether greed motivated them by asking how much they would like to profit more than the other companies. Second, we assessed if fear was their primary motivation by asking how worried they were that other companies might try to cut large amounts of timber each year. Finally, we assessed participants' desire to consume resources by asking how many of the 100 available forested acres they would bid to harvest.

Participants who had written about death (and presumably had their insecurities raised) became more materialistic. They bid for almost 62 of the 100 available acres, whereas those in the control condition bid significantly less—49 acres. Furthermore, participants who wrote about death were significantly more motivated by greed, in that they wanted to profit more than the other companies.

This study is, to my knowledge, the first time a true experiment has been conducted on insecurity and materialism. Past work linking the two was always correlational, limiting our ability to be sure that insecurity is one of the causative factors at work. In contrast, these experimental procedures provide the strongest data thus far that feelings of insecurity actually produce materialistic tendencies.

Summary

Many different types of studies show that when needs for security, safety, and sustenance are not fully satisfied, people place a strong focus on materialistic values and desires. Whether we examine the characteristics of people's parents, family, or nation, or whether we look at the content of dreams or reactions to death, the evidence is the same. Certainly other sources of insecurity must exist that future research will document as leading to a strong value placed on materialistic aims.

My understanding of the connection among insecurity, a materialistic value orientation, and well-being is that sometimes people experience circumstances (nonnurturing parents, poverty, death anxiety) that lead them to feel insecure. This causes unhappiness and dissatisfaction, as security needs must be satisfied for good psychological health. At the same time, insecurity also makes it likely that people will pursue materialistic aims, as both inner predispositions and external consumer culture suggest that resources can purchase security. Thus, materialistic values are both a symptom of an underlying insecurity and a coping strategy taken on in an attempt to alleviate problems and satisfy needs.

The problem is that materialistic values are rather poor coping strategies. As with other coping strategies that may make people feel good in the short term (self-isolation, denial of the problem, hedonistic pleasures such as drinking or sex), materialistic pursuits may in the long term actually maintain and deepen feelings of insecurity. Negative associations between materialistic values and well-being certainly suggest that such a coping strategy is not especially useful in alleviating people's problems. Perhaps it even makes people's problems worse. This seems quite possible, as we will see in the next three chapters, because these values lead people into experiences that work against the satisfaction of other important needs.

5

Fragile Self-Worth

Before Silicon Graphics, Clark said a fortune of $10 million would make him happy; before Netscape, $100 million; before Healtheon, a billion; now, he told Lewis, "Once I have more money than Larry Ellison, I'll be satisfied." Ellison, the founder of the software company Oracle, is worth $13 billion.
—Quotation concerning Jim Clark, founder of Netscape and other computer companies.[1]

Almost everyone believes that getting what you want makes you feel good about yourself and your life. Common wisdom, as well as many psychological theories, says that if we reach our goals, our self-esteem and satisfaction with life should consequently rise. As can be seen in the case of Jim Clark, however, people who are wildly successful in their attempts to attain money and status often remain unfulfilled once they have reached their goal. Clark made his first fortune, but that was not gratifying. Even one billion dollars does not appear to be enough. Instead, only when he makes thirteen billion will he be happy. I suspect that, should Clark reach that goal, he will quickly become dissatisfied and strive for even more money.

Similar processes are probably at work for the rest of us, whose desires are generally more modest than to have wealth surpassing that of some small nations. We may want a raise, a new car, or greater status. We may even succeed in reaching these goals. Yet evidence suggests that, beyond having enough money to meet our basic needs for food, shelter, and the like, attaining wealth, possessions, and status does not yield long-term increases in our happiness or well-being. Even the successful pursuit of materialistic ideals typically turns out to be empty and unsatisfying.

Consider, for example, the research of Edward Diener, who followed the happiness and life satisfaction of almost 5000 United States adults over a nine-year period.[2] Some of these adults experienced large increases in wealth over the nine years, some had only moderate increases, and others barely kept up with the rising cost of living. Regardless, changes in income were not significant predictors of individuals' current happiness and life satisfaction.

Another evocative demonstration of the fact that increases in wealth do not bring about increases in happiness comes from Philip Brickman's study of lottery winners.[3] Twenty-two individuals who had recently won large amounts of money in the Illinois state lottery were compared with a control group of people who lived near the recently rich individuals. All study participants were asked about their general happiness and how much pleasure they derived from everyday experiences, such as talking with a friend, eating breakfast, hearing a funny joke, and the like. The happiness of lottery winners was no different from that of people who had not experienced a large increase in their wealth, and the lottery winners actually reported being *less* pleased with everyday events.

This pattern is repeated yet again in national trends. As mentioned in chapter 1, David Myers reports that as the United States' gross domestic product has expanded over the last few decades, people's happiness has remained constant.[4] Figure 5.1 shows that while the United States economy grew incredibly from 1956 to 1998, doubling most citizens' income, life satisfaction remained almost constant across the same time span. Others have reported similar results in European nations and Japan.[5]

Research yields similar findings when people rate their attainment or progress at materialistic goals. In one such project, Richard Ryan and I asked college students at the University of Rochester and Montana State University to rate how much they felt they had attained materialistic goals (money, fame, image) and nonmaterialistic goals (personal growth, close relationships, community contribution).[6] From these ratings we created four groups of people: those high in attainment of both types of goals; those high only in nonmaterialistic goals; those high only in materialistic goals; and those who felt unsuccessful in reaching either type of goals. We compared the groups in terms of personal well-being, drug use, and self-esteem, among other things.

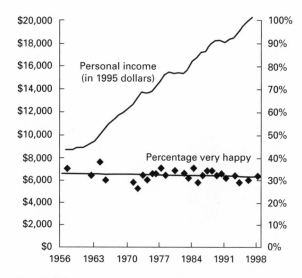

Figure 5.1
Economic growth and life satisfaction in the United States. (From Myers, 2000. Reprinted by permission of the American Psychological Association.)

Figure 5.2 presents the well-being scores of the four groups of subjects in the Rochester sample. Attaining materialistic goals was not very beneficial to well-being. Compare, for example, the first two bars in figure 5.2. Almost equivalent well-being was reported by members of groups 1 and 2. Note also that well-being was quite low for members of group 3. In fact, group 3's well-being was not significantly different from group 4's.

These results were essentially the same for the Montana students and for other measures of psychological health (drug use, self-esteem). Furthermore, these results were replicated in a sample of Russian students, showing again that attaining materialistic pursuits yields little in the way of well-being benefits, and that if they constitute a person's primary attainments, well-being is rather low.[7]

Parallel results occur when tracking the progress that people make in achieving different types of goals over the course of a couple of months. Ken Sheldon and I asked university students about their goals for the coming semester using the personal goal methodology described in chapter 2.[8] Recall that with this method students write down their goals for

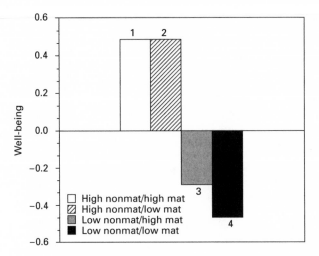

Figure 5.2
Subjective well-being of four groups of college students differing in their reported attainment of materialistic and non-materialistic aspirations. (From Kasser and Ryan, 2001.)

the upcoming months and then rate the extent to which they believe success at these goals will help take them toward materialistic outcomes, as opposed to other outcomes. In this particular study, participants' subjective progress toward their goals was assessed every five days and related to changes in their well-being. Participants' well-being was compared at the beginning of the study, in October, with their responses to the same surveys two months later. Every fifth day they also completed a diary report of their current well-being. In this way we could see if progress at materialistic goals improved well-being from day to day, and from October to December.

Making progress toward materialistic goals did not improve participants' well-being at either the daily or monthly level. Figure 5.3 shows these results for the longer-term changes in well-being. The positively sloped line demonstrates that making little progress toward personal growth and improving one's close relationships (i.e., nonmaterialistic goals) decreased personal well-being, whereas getting closer to such goals increased it. This is what we expected, as making progress toward non-materialistic goals typically satisfies one's needs and thus improves well-

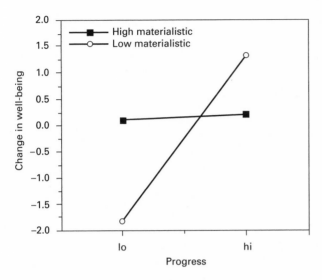

Figure 5.3
Changes in well-being as a function of progress at materialistic and nonmaterialistic goals. (Modified from Sheldon and Kasser, 1998. Reprinted by permission of Sage Publishers.)

being. Of greater interest to the current proposition, people who made progress toward materialistic goals showed no well-being benefits over the course of the semester, as can be seen by the flat line in figure 5.3. That is, the well-being of those who made progress at materialistic goals did not increase relative to two months earlier and was no better than that of people who failed to make progress toward materialistic goals. When we made a similar graph for changes in short-term well-being, it looked essentially the same: making progress in materialistic goals showed no increases in well-being from one day to the next.

Each of these studies reveals that beyond the point of providing for food, shelter, and safety, increases in wealth do little to improve people's well-being and happiness. The implications of this for a materialistic orientation are deep. First, when people follow materialistic values and organize their lives around attaining wealth and possessions, they are essentially wasting their time as far as well-being is concerned. By concentrating on such a profitless style of life, they leave themselves little opportunity to pursue goals that could fulfill their needs and improve the quality of their lives. These arguments are more fully developed in chapters 6 and 7.

The fact that successful pursuit of materialistic values does not yield concomitant increases in well-being also suggests that people's needs for self-esteem and competence are not being satisfied. That is, most psychologists believe that when people attain their goals, their self-esteem and feelings of competence should increase. As we will see in this chapter, however, this does not appear to be the case for people who are particularly focused on materialistic goals. Such individuals often have low self-esteem and believe that their worth depends on their accomplishments and others' praise. Consequently, their sense of esteem is frequently threatened, and their feelings of competence and worthiness are tenuous, even when they succeed. In addition, people with strong materialistic value orientations experience persistent discrepancies between their current states and where they would most like to be. Such chronic gaps between ideals and actual situations can lead to less positive feelings about oneself, and thus less happiness.

Problems with Self-Esteem

Self-esteem is understood by most psychologists to be based on people's evaluations of themselves. When people have high self-esteem, they have more positive than negative self-evaluations, say they feel good about themselves, and believe they are worthy and valuable. In contrast, people with low self-esteem have more negative than positive evaluations about themselves, feel unworthy and unloved, and feel inadequate.

Thousands of studies have been conducted to understand the role of self-esteem in people's lives, and psychologists have discovered a great deal about the benefits of high self-esteem, as well as the environments that support or hinder its development.[9] In brief, high self-esteem comes in part from growing up in a warm environment with loving parents and from successfully using one's competencies and abilities to attain one's goals. Low self-esteem occurs when people are neglected and belittled, and when they feel unable to get what they want.

Recall from chapter 4 that people strongly focused on materialistic values were often raised in nonnurturing environments that poorly satisfied their needs for security and safety. Because such environments also typically diminish people's self-esteem, it is not surprising that materialistic values are associated with low self-esteem. For example, college students in the United States and England who are highly focused on materialistic values reported feeling bad about themselves, agreeing with statements such as, "I certainly feel useless at times," and "At times I think I am no good at all."[10] We cannot be sure whether people with chronically low self-esteem adopt materialistic values (perhaps as a way to overcome feelings of insecurity) or whether materialistic values cause low self-esteem (as suggested later in this chapter), but it is clear that a connection between them exists.

Although low self-esteem is clearly problematic, psychologists recognize that positive evaluations about ourselves do not always signal a *healthy* sense of esteem. Sometimes when we say good things about ourselves, we are actually covering up a rather fragile, unstable sense of self-esteem. Think, for example, of the braggart who loves recounting his exploits and talks of no one more highly than himself. Often deeper insecurity and concerns that he is not really as good as he says he is underlie such inflated self-evaluations.

This fragile, unstable self-esteem is called "contingent" by some theorists.[11] Contingent self-esteem occurs when people's sense of worth depends on meeting particular external standards. For example, when people feel that their self-worth hinges on the grade they receive on a test, whether or not they close a big business deal, how many papers they publish in a year, or how much they weigh, their self-esteem is contingent on external rewards or feedback. When such individuals are successful at meeting their goals (they get an A, they make a million dollars, etc.), they experience positive feelings about themselves and their accomplishments. Such positive feelings tend to be short-lived, however, and the sense of worth is fairly unstable, as new challenges and threats quickly arise that can easily deflate their self-esteem. And if people do not receive the positive external feedback required by contingent self-esteem, their evaluations of themselves can plummet.

Contingent self-esteem clearly shares much in common with how materialistic values are conceived. As stated in chapter 2, values for money, image, and fame cluster together because they all focus on extrinsic concerns. Thus, people with materialistic values hinge their self-esteem and self-worth on whether they have attained some reward (money) or whether other people praise them (say they look good, admire them, etc.). The overlap between materialistic values and contingent self-esteem is also evident in some of the items from the Richins and Dawson materialism scale. As shown in table 2.5, people strongly oriented toward materialism agree with items such as, "The things I own say a lot about how well I'm doing in life," and "I'd be happier if I could afford to buy more things." When people believe that their worth depends on external signifiers such as money and status, they are much more easily buffeted by the whims of fate than when they have a secure, stable, and deep sense of esteem that is not dependent on such accomplishments.

Contingent self-esteem is also prominent in one of the psychological problems that occurs with materialistic values, namely, narcissism. Many social critics claim that narcissism is the disorder of our materialistic society, and some psychodynamic theorists note that it often develops as a defense against low self-esteem.[12] According to these theorists, narcissists attempt to cover their feelings of inadequacy by going to the opposite extreme, hiding behind a false sense of worth that is typically dependent on external accomplishments.

An excellent example of the narcissism and contingent sense of self-worth frequently accompanying materialistic values comes from the dream of one highly materialistic young man who participated in the study cited earlier.[13] The following is his dream in its entirety.

It all started at the U.S. Grand Prix in Lagunaseca, CA. The first day of practice with the 250cc bikes and I walk up to the Honda team owner and tell him that I can beat anyone here. He and all the people around him bust up laughing. Then I present him with the ultimatum, "Give me a bike and I prove it!" First, he thinks, no way am I going to let some stranger take one of my $50,000 motorcycles out and destroy it. Then, after more boasting by me, he decides to let me take out one of the back-up bikes. After 2 laps of warming up the tires, I go on to set a track record for fastest lap. Well the Honda team is shocked, "Where did this guy come from, who is he, why hasn't he been racing all this time?" Well they decide to let me try to qualify for the race, and I tell them that I don't want the pole-position, but prefer 2nd or 3rd start on the grid. They start to laugh again. When it comes time for qualifying though my times are only hundredths of a second off pole. This puts me right in second start next to Max Biaggi on pole, Doriano Romboni in 3rd position, and another Honda rider in fourth. The race begins with me following Biaggi in the front and then, two laps later, passing him for first. After the pass, I never look back and win the race by a full ten seconds over Max. After receiving the trophy and hundreds of questions from reporters, the team owner offers me a ride for the rest of the season, in which I place second in points due to a late start in the season. World Championship doesn't come until next year when I race the whole season.

This man's dream contains frequent mention of being great, the best, and a champion. His boastful behavior toward the Honda owner reflects his attempt to appear to others as very competent, and he revels in the rewards and recognition he receives. From my viewpoint, this focus on competence and public attainment of materialistic rewards belies a contingent sense of self-worth, in which the basis of this man's positive feelings about himself depend on the praise and feedback of others. Such a fragile, unstable self-esteem is unlikely to provide materialistic individuals with a deeper feeling of worth and a high quality of life, however.

Never-Ending Discrepancies

Another way in which materialistic individuals may have difficulty in fulfilling their needs for esteem and competence derives from discrepancies. Many psychologists believe that people's emotional states are largely a function of how far they are from who, what, or where they ideally would like to be.[14] Discrepancies can apply to almost any aspect of people's lives, including their bodies, personalities, and relationships. Perhaps one woman wants straight hair even though hers is curly; perhaps a man wishes he were more outgoing instead of so shy; perhaps another woman wishes her spouse talked to her more and watched less football. Regardless of the particular ideals people strive for, when they want things that they do not have, a discrepancy arises, making them feel sad, anxious, guilty, angry, or dissatisfied. Discrepancies also motivate people to engage in behaviors designed to reduce the gap between actual and ideal (buy hair-straightening products, talk to people more, discuss the situation with one's husband). But if the discrepancy is chronic, or if people feel unable to resolve it, needs for esteem and competence can remain unfulfilled.

The ideals that people strive for, and that thus partly determine discrepancies, come from a number of sources. Personal values are one obvious source, as, by definition, values are what people view as the best goals or as their personal concept of desirable. People also develop ideals by looking at the lives of their friends, neighbors, co-workers, and relatives. This is of course the old idea of keeping up with the Joneses. A great deal of information about what is ideal also comes from our culture. Cultures have always encouraged certain ideals through their educational, religious, and political systems, and contemporary culture is no different.

For people oriented toward materialistic values, each of these sources can lead to the formation of ideals concerning money, possessions, looks, and status. Naturally, their values direct them to seek out such ideals. In addition, because people strongly oriented toward materialistic values believe that wealth, attractiveness, and status are ideals, they are especially attuned to information in their environments that reinforces this notion. That is, just as a hungry person notes the smell of fresh bread while walking down a street, materialistic individuals are alert to signs of wealth, status, and image in people with whom they interact and images they notice in the world. And never before has such a veritable megamarket of images existed on which a materialist might gorge. The Joneses next door have the fancy, popular vehicle of the moment, they regularly travel to exotic destinations, their children wear the best sneakers and have the latest computer games, and on and on. Articles, images, and advertisements on television, radio, highways, and the Internet proclaim how much happier life would be with this product or that image. Having materialistic ideals is almost overdetermined by circumstances of contemporary life.

Several lines of research suggest, however, that these ideals lead us frequently to experience discrepancies, and thus dissatisfaction. At least two processes are involved. First, materialistic ideals often romanticize wealth and possessions, in part because commercials present a far rosier picture of the materialistic lifestyle than is actually the case. To the extent that these unreachable ideals become ours, chronic discrepancies are likely to result. Second, even if we do reach such ideals, we are not likely to find that our quality of life has improved. As a result, we may form even higher materialistic ideals, creating new discrepancies and further dissatisfaction. Both of these vicious cycles not only maintain a materialistic lifestyle, they also lead to poor fulfillment of needs for competence and esteem, and thus to greater dissatisfaction.

Too Ideal

Consider an individual whose goal is to make a million dollars. This is what she conceives of as ideal, having been exposed throughout her life to countless messages claiming that wealth is the primary sign of success, and that the purchase of particular goods and services will make her life meaningful and happy. At the moment, she is worth only about $100,000 and, instead of living in the lap of luxury, she works long hours at a job she does not particularly like, commuting forty-five minutes each way in her six-year-old sedan to and from her comfortable but far from opulent single-family dwelling in the suburbs. Clearly this woman has a discrepancy in her life and, to the extent that her materialistic ideals are central, she is probably dissatisfied. This dissatisfaction motivates her to pursue her materialistic ideals even more strongly, which perpetuates her value system and her unhappiness.

Although no single study, to my knowledge, has yet simultaneously verified all the links in this cycle, empirical research does exist that supports each individual link. And as I will show, this vicious cycle can operate even when people's ideals are less immoderate than extreme wealth.

To begin, materialistic individuals seem to have overly inflated, unrealistic ideas about the worth of wealth and possessions. For example, Shivani Khanna and I asked United States students about qualities that characterize wealthy individuals.[15] Respondents with strong materialistic values were likely to believe that a significant majority of rich people were "smart," "cultured," and "successful in everything." Such inflated ideals about what it means to be wealthy likely set up discrepancies for materialists, most of whom will feel they fall short when they assess these qualities in themselves.

One of the main reasons materialistic individuals have unrealistic ideals about wealth and possessions is that they frequently view such images in the media. In searching out messages that reinforce their value system, they spend many hours watching one primary agent of this value system: television. Research studies using different materialism scales and conducted with individuals in Australia, Denmark, Finland, Hong Kong, India, and the United States have shown that materialistic individuals watch a great deal of television.[16] Although this fact is interesting in some other regards (as we will see in chapter 7), the main point here is that the minds of materialistic people become saturated with shows and ads exhibiting levels of attractiveness and wealth well above the norm, and thus beyond the level of attainment of the average viewer.

In particular, advertisements on television (and elsewhere) are specifically designed to present idealized images of people who own or use a particular product, in the hope that by pairing these images with the product, viewers will be convinced to purchase the product.[17] We see that a newly improved laundry detergent has better chemicals that our older, dull detergent lacks, and that the woman who uses this detergent has a family pleased with their crisp, clean clothes; whereas, our family never has a word to say about their washed clothes, except to complain. We see that this year's new cars have many improved features compared with our automobile—although it is only two years old—and that people who drive these new cars live in nice neighborhoods, travel to fun places, and have sexy, happy spouses. Put in terms of discrepancy theory, ads create an image (being like the person in the ad who has the product and a great life) that is different from our actual state (being ourself, sans product, with an average life). Marketers and businesspeople are banking that advertisement-induced discrepancies will convince us to buy the new improved detergent or take out a lease on the new car, so that our discrepancies can be reduced, and so their bank accounts can be enlarged.

The consequences of believing that the wealthy have wonderful lives and of frequently viewing idealized ads are that people become frustrated with their current state and thus less happy. In a series of studies, Joseph Sirgy, H. Lee Meadow, and Don Rahtz have explored the interrelations of materialism, television, discrepancies, and life satisfaction.[18] In some of this early work, conducted with large samples of elderly Americans, people who watched a lot of television reported low satisfaction with their lives and low overall morale, and also compared themselves unfavorably with other "people in your position." Watching television presumably made viewers feel that they measured up less favorably than other people because they could not live up to what they saw on television; thus, they experienced increased discrepancies and low overall life satisfaction.

In another project, Sirgy, Meadow, Rahtz and their colleagues surveyed over 1,200 adults from the United States, Canada, Australia, China, and

Turkey about life satisfaction, their levels of materialism (using the Richins and Dawson scale), and the extent to which they watched television.[19] Participants also reported how favorably they felt in comparison with people they saw on television by responding to statements such as, "I am more well off financially than most people shown on television commercials," and "I consider my family to be lower class compared to the typical family they show on television." Finally, participants expressed how satisfied they were in general and with their standard of living or income on the whole.

People with a strong materialistic orientation were likely to watch a lot of television, compare themselves unfavorably with people they saw on television, be dissatisfied with their standard of living, and have low life satisfaction. Using a statistical technique called structural equation modeling, the investigators showed that by watching a great deal of television, materialistic individuals are exposed to images of wealth and beauty that make them dissatisfied with their current economic state. This dissatisfaction with the material realm of their lives "spills over" into their overall sense of satisfaction with their entire life. Of note, most of the support for these results came from the United States sample.

Another series of studies further showed that discrepancies form in reaction to overidealized advertising images by evaluating how college women respond to ads with extremely attractive models.[20] In the first of these studies, Marsha Richins interviewed college women to determine whether they compared themselves with models in ads, and how such comparisons made them feel. Many students mentioned that they frequently looked through magazines as a way to envision what they might ideally look like. For example, one woman said, "There's certain [ads] that I look at and say, 'Wow! I'd sure like to look like that.' " Yet some also reported that unpleasant feelings result from comparing themselves with these images. One woman reflected, "You look at these ads and you feel inadequate, like you can't measure up."

In the next two experiments, Richins showed advertisements to over 200 undergraduate women. Half of the participants looked at ads for perfume and sportswear in which extremely attractive female models appeared and the other half saw ads for similar products that did not include any people. After looking at the ads, the women rated how attractive they believed themselves to be and how satisfied they were with their attractiveness. Women who viewed the advertisements with models reported less satisfaction with their own attractiveness, but did not differ from the control group in self-ratings of how attractive they thought themselves to be. This suggests that the ads did not change the women's assessment of their actual attractiveness, but raised their ideals about attractiveness in general. The consequence of an increasing gap between their own attractiveness and what they viewed as ideal (because of the women in the ads) was increased dissatisfaction with their own looks.

Although this experiment examined only one particular type of ad and one particular type of self-relevant discrepancy, its implications are much broader. The results suggest that decreased life satisfaction could be a side effect of frequent exposure to all the different types of idealized images in the media, whether for cars, furniture, or baby powder.

We have seen thus far that materialistic individuals are likely to over-idealize wealth and possessions, and as a result, they are likely to be dissatisfied with aspects of their life, as their actual state cannot measure up to their ideals. The next step in the cycle occurs when this discrepancy drives people to engage in further materialistic behavior. Evidence for this comes from a set of experiments in which Ottmar Braun and Robert Wicklund tested whether people lay claim to materialistic status symbols when they feel that their identity is incomplete (their actual state is below their ideal).[21] In one study, first-year United States college students were more likely to report owning articles displaying the name of their university than were fourth-year students. Similarly, inexperienced German adult tennis players were more likely to prefer certain brands of tennis clothing than were experienced tennis players. In both cases, less experienced individuals were likely to feel that they had not yet reached their ideals (graduation, proficiency in tennis); as a result, they compensated by possessing material symbols to bolster their identity.

In two experiments Braun and Wicklund actually made people feel incomplete in their identities. In one experiment, German law students were randomly assigned to answer questions that made it clear that they had not yet successfully reached their goals; that is, to become lawyers. For example, they were asked about their years of experience, how many conventions they had attended, how many papers they had published, and so on. Participants in the control group were asked about more routine matters unlikely to heighten awareness of the discrepancy between their ideal and actual states. Next, all subjects reported where they were going on vacation the coming summer and rated how prestigious and "in fashion" their vacation spot was. Students who felt committed to becoming lawyers (really wanted the goal) and who had been made aware of the discrepancy between their actual and ideal states were especially likely to report that their vacation spot was prestigious and in fashion. This was not the case for students who were uncommitted to becoming lawyers or who were not made more aware of the discrepancy. This study was conceptually replicated by a similar experiment with German business students.

What these results show is that when people realize that they have not reached an ideal they hold, they desire material means of conspicuously demonstrating that they are in fact high-status, worthy individuals. This is compatible with the argument presented in chapter 4 about the ways people who feel insecure sometimes compensate by pursuing materialistic aims. Furthermore, it provides the final piece of evidence for the vicious cycle outlined above: materialistic people overidealize wealth and possessions and therefore experience discrepancies that cause them to feel dissatisfied and to want further materialistic means of feeling good about themselves. But the satisfactions from this compensation only temporarily improve their sense of worth, and soon they return to another cycle of dissatisfaction.

Rising Baselines

Consider another hypothetical individual whose goal is to make a million dollars. Let us say that he actually succeeds. No doubt he will experience some positive emotions on reaching his goal and will esteem himself as a result. As we saw at the beginning of this chapter, however, his rising income is unlikely to improve his happiness and satisfaction with life. Thus, he will, in not too long a time, recognize that he is no happier or more satisfied than he was before. Furthermore, as his lifestyle becomes that of a millionaire, he will habituate to his more lavish surroundings and begin to compare himself with people who have even more money.

It is probably difficult for the average person to imagine becoming accustomed to a yacht, servants, and limousines, but consider how you would feel if you could never take a hot shower again. Many people in wealthier nations have become used to this pleasure and actually think of it as a necessity. Actually, a hot shower is clearly a luxury, especially when we consider that most of the world's population has never experienced such a pleasure. What has happened is that this material pleasure has become the new baseline, the new current state that we want to improve. With this in mind, it becomes understandable how J. Paul Getty can quip, "A billion dollars doesn't go as far as it used to."[22] When a person is accustomed to having several million dollars for a rainy day and thinks nothing of spending hundreds of thousands of dollars on whatever he or she wishes, even a billion dollars can become boringly routine.

Research in fact indicates that once people become used to a certain standard of living, it becomes the baseline from which they compare themselves to others. Arie Kapteyn and Tom Wansbeek showed this by asking people from a number of income brackets how much money they "required" to meet their minimum needs.[23] It was no surprise that wealthier individuals felt that they required more than did poorer people. Wealthy people's sense of what was absolutely necessary was higher because their lifestyle was their norm.

Returning to our hypothetical millionaire, after the initial glow of attaining his goal wears off, he will likely find himself feeling rather ho-hum about it. The new luxuries he purchases will become his new norm, and because they are empty of true satisfaction anyhow, he will probably experience a lingering sense of dissatisfaction. "What's the problem?" he may wonder. Being oriented toward materialistic values, he will most likely decide that the problem is that he still does not have enough money or possessions, and so the logical thing to do is to strive for two or even ten million dollars. A new discrepancy is thus formed, causing new dissatisfactions, which will be temporarily alleviated only if and when this new ideal is attained. Alas, even achieving the new goal will again only temporarily solve these feelings of dissatisfaction, as our multimillionaire's sense of self-worth is most likely contingent on his external worth and his relative standing to those even wealthier than he is.

In this respect, the desire for material goods, fame, and attractiveness is like drug addiction, a parallel pointed to by other theorists.[24] Just as an alcoholic who first got a buzz from three beers eventually requires six, and then nine, and then a whole case before feeling drunk, a person strongly oriented toward materialistic values might originally experience a "high" from a small purchase or paycheck, but will eventually require more and bigger possessions and sums before the equivalent positive feelings occur. People thus become obsessed with possessions and money, looking for the next new thing that will give them the temporary fix they no longer can receive from their old things. As they form ever higher materialistic goals, they experience new and unpleasant discrepancies. Through this process, their needs for feeling good about what they have and who they are remain relatively unfulfilled.

Summary

The arguments and data in this chapter show that successfully pursuing materialistic goals fails to increase one's happiness. When people and nations make progress in their materialistic ambitions, they may experience some temporary improvement of mood, but it is likely to be short-lived and superficial. Furthermore, some of the psychological dynamics related to the strong pursuit of materialistic goals (problems with self-esteem and discrepancies) keep individuals' well-being from improving as their wealth and status increase. The sad truth is that when people feel the emptiness of either material success or failure, they often persist in thinking that more will be better, and thus continue to strive for what will never make them happier. In the process, they receive relatively poor satisfaction of their needs for competence and esteem, fail to correct the underlying psychological issues that lead them to such an empty pursuit in the first place, and ignore other important psychological needs (as discussed in the next two chapters), all to the detriment of their well-being.

6

Poor Relationships

Money is my first, last, and only love.
—Armand Hammer[1]

To say that humans are social creatures is about as newsworthy as saying that we breathe. Our lives unfold in a social matrix that is both deep and wide, and our interactions with other people and the culture at large affect our personalities and behavior in many ways. Consequently, many psychologists agree that good interpersonal relationships and involvement in one's community form two cornerstones of personal well-being. To give even an abbreviated list of theorists and researchers who believe that high-quality connections with others are necessary for psychological health would take quite a few pages of this book.[2] But it is clear from this corpus of work that our psychological health depends in part on whether we feel close and connected with other people, and on whether we can give and receive love, care, and support.

People who focus on materialistic aims often do so at the "expense" of their relationships, however. Many thinkers and social critics have commented on this phenomenon. Sociologist Robert D. Putnam recently documented the decline of civic engagement in America, reflected in decreasing participation in bowling leagues, community organizations, and so on.[3] Political scientist Robert E. Lane similarly commented that people in capitalistic countries suffer "a kind of famine of warm interpersonal relationships, of easy-to-reach neighbors, of encircling, inclusive memberships, and of solid family life."[4] What these and other thinkers note is that materialistic values "crowd out" other meaningful pursuits, as the time we "spend" earning and consuming often means neglect of our spouses, children, friends, and community.

Some data have been presented showing that materialistic values are indeed associated with a number of problems concerning connections to other people. As reviewed in chapter 2, people who highly value materialistic pursuits are rated by interviewers as being less adapted to society and as exhibiting more antisocial behaviors. As described in the Cohens' research, materialistic values are associated with several personality disorders characterized by difficulties in relationships. Schizoid, schizotypal, and avoidant individuals have difficulty forming relationships; borderline and narcissistic individuals are often self-centered in their interactions with others; and paranoid individuals show difficulties with trust. All of these findings point to poor relationships as one possible explanation for why materialistic values and low psychological well-being occur together.

As a way of more directly examining the relationships of materialistic individuals, Rich Ryan and I asked over 200 students attending Montana State University about both their materialistic tendencies (as measured by the Aspiration Index) and about their most important love relationship and friendships in general.[5] First, participants reported how long their longest love relationship and friendship had lasted. Next, they described these relationships using a series of adjectives, some of which reflected positive characteristics such as trust, acceptance, and friendship, and others of which reflected negative qualities, including jealousy and emotional extremes. To measure the overall quality of participants' connections to other people, the length and quality of their relationships were combined into indices of relationship quality for both friends and lovers. Students who strongly focused on the pursuit of wealth, fame, and image reported lower-quality relationships with friends and lovers. That is, materialistic values were associated with shorter, less positive, and more negative relationships than were nonmaterialistic values.

This finding is echoed in the results of a study investigating aggressive tendencies in dating relationships. Ken Sheldon and Mindy Flanagan gave 500 students the Aspiration Index and a scale measuring how often in the last six months they had engaged in a variety of different behaviors with their romantic partner.[6] These ranged from arguing, insulting, and swearing at their partner to pushing, grabbing, shoving, and physically hurting their partner. Even after statistically controlling for subjects' preexisting levels of aggressive tendencies, materialistic values were associated with more conflictual and aggressive behaviors in dating relationships.

Other studies find that materialistic individuals experience more alienation in their social relationships than nonmaterialistic people. Sometimes people feel able to connect with others in their society and free to express themselves in their relationships, whereas at other times they feel separated, disconnected, and pressured to be like someone else in order to be accepted and liked. In one study, Shivani Khanna and I asked subjects how much they agreed with statements such as, "In order to relate to others, I often have to put on a mask," "I often feel detached from my social environment," and "I often feel like I have to perform for others." Both Indian and United States students who were highly focused on materialistic pursuits (as measured by the Aspiration Index, the Richins and Dawson scale, and another scale developed by George Moschis) reported feelings of alienation and separateness from society.[7] John McHoskey has reported similar results in a sample of seventy undergraduates in Michigan; students highly focused on financial success were likely to feel estranged from their culture. Specifically, they frequently felt that their "ideas and opinions about important matters" differed from those of their relatives and friends, and from religious and national norms.[8]

Evidence of an association between problematic relationships and materialistic values is also revealed at a more unconscious level. In our study of dreams, my wife and I found that people highly oriented toward materialistic values often avoided intimacy and connection in their dreams.[9] Many participants, both high and low in materialistic value orientation, reported dreams of conflict or problems with their romantic partners. Whereas people with low materialistic values typically tried to use these dreamed conflicts or difficulties as ways to improve communication or relationships, those with high materialistic values showed the opposite tendency. For example, a woman who had recurring dreams in which her boyfriend was unfaithful to her reflected, "I'm always crabby at my boyfriend for something he did in a stupid dream . . . I guess I question what he did the night of the dream just to be sure—but it never gets me anywhere." Other participants highly focused on materialism seemed to be rather traumatized by past relationships and now shied away from intimacy. One woman dreamed of a former boyfriend who died in a car accident; she wrote, "His image still I keep in my heart. His sad eyes in the dream still hang in my mind. I couldn't go on a date or do something like that because I didn't want to be unfaithful to him," despite the fact she had actually broken up with him not long before his accident. Similarly, a man who dreamed of being reunited on a playground with his ex-girlfriend reflected that his dream "made me realize that this girl meant too much to me. That possibly true love is not attainable, and that I'm not ready for another relationship . . . It [the dream] led me to be less trusting of others and I've realized not to get attached to others [sic]. I won't get into another relationship that's so serious." Even at an unconscious level, individuals with a strong materialistic value orientation often flee from intimacy and closeness.

In sum, compared to those who care little for materialism, people who hold materialistic aims as central to their values have shorter, more conflictual relationships with friends and lovers, feel alienated and disconnected from others in society, and have dreams in which they move away from intimate connections with others.

What is it about materialistic values that leads to such difficulties in relationships? At least two processes are probably at work. First, strongly materialistic people often devalue close, intimate relationships and community involvement. Thus, they sometimes neglect their relationships, and care little about having healthy relationships. Second, materialistic values appear to bleed over into relationships, tainting them in ways that damage the quality of connectedness and decrease the ability to satisfy needs for intimacy, closeness, and connection.

Valuing Connectedness

Evidence from several investigations substantiates the claim that when people highly value wealth, possessions, status, and image, the emphasis they place on interpersonal relationships and contributions to their community declines. Work conducted with the Aspiration Index consistently supports this fact. Specifically, materialistic people are less invested in goals such as, "I will express my love for special people," "I will have a committed, intimate relationship," "I will help others improve their lives," and "I will work for the betterment of society." Similarly, teens in the Cohens' study who placed a high priority on being rich tended to have a relatively low concern with taking "care of others who need me." Research in the United States and Singapore shows that, compared to those scoring low on materialism, adults who score high on Richins and Dawson's scale care less about "warm relationships with others," friendship, and love.[10]

Even stronger evidence that materialistic values oppose connectedness derives from the work of Shalom Schwartz, who has collected data on values from adults, college students, and teachers in forty nations around the world.[11] Participants rated the importance of a long list of values, which were analyzed using a statistical technique that locates the values in a circular space. Values that end up close to one another in this "circumplex" are those most people experience as relatively compatible with each other, whereas values at opposite sides of the circle are those experienced by most people as contradictory or in conflict with each other.

Although materialistic values were not explicitly measured, several individual values cohered into a grouping quite similar to what other researchers consider to be materialistic tendencies. Specifically, values for wealth, social recognition, preserving public image, being ambitious, and being successful all lay fairly close to each other in the circumplex, reflecting their compatibility with each other. What's more, analyses showed that these values directly opposed two social values: benevolence and universalism. Benevolence is concerned with the "preservation and enhancement of the welfare of people with whom one is in frequent personal contact," and includes valuing the characteristics of being loyal, responsible, honest, forgiving, and helpful, and of desiring true friendship and mature love. Universalism involves "understanding, appreciation, tolerance, and protection for the welfare of *all* people and for nature" (emphasis in original) and includes social justice, world at peace, equality, and being broad-minded. Schwartz's cross-cultural evidence, compiled from thousands of individuals sampled in most parts of the globe, shows that something about materialism conflicts with valuing the characteristics of strong relationships (loyalty, helpfulness, love) and with caring about the broader community (peace, justice, equality).[12]

Experiments with preschoolers complement these findings. Marvin Goldberg and Gerald Gorn explored whether watching advertisements might lead children to become less concerned with socially oriented activities.[13] Four- and five-year-old children were randomly assigned to watch a ten-minute program that contained either no commercials or two commercials for a particular toy. Children were then shown pictures of two equally attractive boys. One of the boys held the toy that had been advertised, but he was described as "not so nice"; the other boy was empty-handed but said to be "a nice boy." Children were asked which boy they would rather play with, and whether they would rather play with the toy or with their friends in a sandbox. Those who had watched the commercials were likely to select the less socially oriented choice. For example, only 30 percent of children who had not seen the commercial wanted to play with the not-so-nice boy, but 65 percent of those who had seen the commercial were willing to play with him so that they might also be able to play with the toy. Similarly, 70 percent of children who had not seen the commercial chose to play with their friends in the sandbox, while only 36 percent of those who had seen the commercial opted for their friends. Thus, in both situations, the children's materialistic yearnings overwhelmed their desire for healthy social interactions.

The conflict between materialistic values and connections to others revealed in these investigations can be explained in a few ways. The different value orientations could reflect two different motivational styles, one oriented toward the satisfaction of psychological needs, and the other toward obtaining rewards and recognition of others. In a parallel manner, Schwartz suggests that pursuing both materialistic values and benevolence-universalism values is likely to bring about strong internal and social conflict, as "acceptance of others as equals and concern for their welfare interferes with the pursuit of one's own relative success and dominance over others."[14] It may also be that materialistic values lead people to view being close to and caring for others as a profitless pursuit, one that will not gain them anything of worth. Indeed, as suggested by the research reviewed in the next section, materialistic values may orient individuals to see other people primarily as means to their own materialistic ends.

People as Objects

Because values have broad effects on human behavior, the extent to which individuals focus on materialistic pursuits affects the way they interact with other people. When people place a strong emphasis on consuming and buying, earning and spending, thinking of the monetary worth of things, and thinking of things a great deal of the time, they may also become more likely to treat people like things. Philosopher Martin Buber referred to this interpersonal stance as I-It relationships, in which others' qualities, subjective experience, feelings, and desires are ignored, seen as unimportant, or viewed only in terms of their usefulness to oneself.[15] In such relationships, other people become reduced to objects, little different from products that may be purchased, used, and discarded as necessary. Buber contrasted this objectifying type of relationship with an I-Thou relationship in which other people are recognized as experiencing entities with subjective feelings and perspectives that may differ from one's own, but are nonetheless just as important.

It is not hard to find examples of I-It relationships and objectification in consumer-driven cultures, as they have become increasingly common. Here are three short examples, showing how parental, romantic, and business relationships can be infiltrated by the beliefs of an objectifying, materialistic mindset.

I saw a short article in an airline magazine about a trend for parents to desire male nannies for their children, as men are assumedly more likely than women to push children to compete, a supposedly desirable skill in today's capitalistic world.[16] The article concluded with a quotation from the president of the Intelligence Factory, "Parents always have to be managing their assets, including their children." Note how children are conceived of as financial appendages of their parents that must be controlled to ensure a positive reflection on their elders, not as individual beings whose own inner predispositions must be nurtured.

We can also see objectification when people talk about dating. In a very telling study, Aaron Ahuvia interviewed twenty-seven clients at a nonprofit dating service, finding that the ways they talked about dating and meeting others were replete with what he called "market metaphors."[17] Clients referred to the dating scene as "seeing fresh meat on a table" or being a "kid in a candy store." Others talked about themselves as a kind of commodity, saying, "There was a time in my life that I would have felt anxiety [about dating] because I didn't feel I had very much to sell"; now this client feels he is "a good product for those who were in that market." Other people used economic metaphors, saying that dating is like "going on a job interview" or "investing in the stock market." Absent is discussion of sharing and caring about others, about trying to get to know someone deeply.

Finally, consider an advertisement I saw for a business negotiating course. It shows two men in suits, separated by a desk. The potential client says, "I can call six people right now who can give me a better price than that." The ad goes on: "If you cut your price to please your client, your boss will scream. He'll call you a wimp. You hate being called a wimp. But the buyer says he doesn't need you. Is it true? Is he bluffing?" We turn inside the brochure, and read, "Every salesperson knows the stress, the worry, the guessing what the other side is thinking . . . Maybe . . . your client refuses to commit, ducking and dodging all your attempts to nail him down. Or he commits, then rakes you over the coals by haggling every little point until your profit is gone—and your patience exhausted." These surely do not constitute the types of interactions that satisfy one's needs for closeness and intimacy. Bosses scream and insult. Clients lie, "duck and dodge," and "rake" one over coals. And the salesperson, feeling worried, stressed, and helpless, replies in kind, trying to "nail down" the client. How much more effective this salesperson could be, according to the ad, if only he participated in the negotiating seminar so he could "come away with a whole arsenal of strategies" and "a whole array of hard-hitting tactics, techniques, and tips." The war imagery is obvious, but the failure to treat each other as human beings is perhaps less so.

These examples suggest that when consumption, possessions, and money become our primary aims, we become less concerned with fully understanding others' subjective experience, feelings, and desires. Instead, others become objects and thus lose value as people. In the materialist mindset, people exist largely to reflect well on ourselves and to be used and manipulated to obtain what we want.

If we take this view, our tendency to treat others with generosity and empathy can decline. The link between materialistic values and nongenerosity was noted by Belk, who measured such feelings as a central component of materialism (see table 2.4). Other studies also link materialistic values to selfish, nongenerous behavior. A sample of United States adults in Richins and Dawson's study were asked to imagine how they would spend a $20,000 windfall. Those scoring high in materialism reported that they would spend an average of $3,445 on "buying things I want or need," over three times as much as low materialists, who imagined spending $1,106 on themselves. High materialists were also less generous than low materialists in terms of how much they would likely give to a church organization or charity ($733 vs. $1,782, respectively) and how much they would give or lend to friends or relatives ($1,089 vs. $2,631). Similar results were found in a sample of undergraduates studied by John McHoskey; individuals with highly central aspirations for financial success were less likely than those with lower materialistic goals to report engaging in helpful, prosocial behaviors such as lending money to someone, tutoring, and doing volunteer work.[18]

Materialistic individuals also care less about the viewpoints of other people. Ken Sheldon and I measured college students' empathy, or ability and willingness to consider the point of view of other people. Empathic people agree with statements such as, "Before criticizing somebody, I try to imagine how I would feel if I were in their place," and disagree with statements such as, "If I'm sure I'm right about something, I don't waste much time listening to other people's arguments." Students focused on materialistic goals showed a relatively low desire to "get into another person's shoes" and instead felt that there was little need to see another's viewpoint.[19]

Failure to be empathic and generous is only one element of objectification, however, and only one part of what damages our relationships when we are highly focused on materialistic values. Other research shows that materialism is also associated with a tendency to use and manipulate others to magnify our own status, image, or personal gain.

Barry Schwartz has called these "instrumental friendships," writing that in capitalist, consumeristic societies "all that is required is that each 'friend' can provide something useful to the other. Instrumental friend-ships come very close to being market-like, contractual relations, with personal contact and the knowledge of mutual interdependence substitut-ing for formal contractual documents."[20] In other words, rather than in-teracting as two people who want to share and connect with each other, friends are used for certain activities or certain desires. To investigate this idea, Shivani Khanna and I assessed individuals' tendencies to use other people in their relationships as a means of enhancing their own popular-ity, status, or esteem.[21] People with a strong tendency toward objectifying others agreed with items such as, "I like to be with 'cool' people because it helps me look 'cool' too," "I like popular people," and "If a friend can't help me get ahead in life, I usually end the friendship." This survey, together with three others measuring materialistic tendencies, were ad-ministered to groups of college students in the United States, India, and Denmark. Substantial associations were found between students' materi-alism scores and their tendency to use others for instrumental purposes, and this was true in all three nations.

Another idea that captures many of the characteristics of objectification is Machiavellianism, after the Italian political strategist. A widely used questionnaire exists to measure this philosophy of life, assessing tenden-cies toward cynicism, distrust of others, and self-centeredness, as well as the desire to manipulate others.[22] People who score high in Machiavelli-anism approve of manipulation in interpersonal relationships (agree with statements such as, "Never tell anyone the real reason you did something unless it is useful to you"), believe that people are essentially lazy and deceptive (agree with statements such as, "Anyone who completely trusts anyone else is asking for trouble"), and care little for honesty (disagree with statements such as, "There is no excuse for lying to someone else"). People high in Machiavellianism are interpersonally cold, have relation-ship problems, and exhibit substantial narcissistic and psychopathic be-haviors, according to research. This personality trait also relates to materialistic values, as shown by McHoskey in three samples of over 250 undergraduates. Individuals highly focused on financial success aspira-tions also scored highly in Machiavellianism.[23]

One study convincingly demonstrated that materialistic values actually lead to manipulative and selfish behavior in social interactions. Ken Shel-

Table 6.1
Social dilemma matrix presented to participants in Sheldon et al. (2000)

	Individual	Group
If all four choose C	Each gets 8	Group gets 32
If 3 choose C and 1 chooses G	Cs get 6, G gets 11	Group gets 29
If 2 choose C and 2 choose G	Cs get 4, Gs get 9	Group gets 26
If 1 chooses C and 3 choose G	C gets 2, Gs get 7	Group gets 23
If all four choose G	Each gets 5	Group gets 20

C, cooperate; G, get ahead.
Reprinted by permission of Aldine de Gruyter.

don, his wife Meli Sheldon, and Richard Osbaldiston investigated what materialistic individuals would do when given the opportunity and motivation either to cooperate with their friends or to try to get ahead of them.[24] Ninety-five first-year college students identified three friends who could fill out some surveys for a study. The original participants and their peers then completed the Aspiration Index and played a social game called the Prisoner's Dilemma. Social dilemma games such as this one are frequently used by scientists to investigate how people interact with each other in situations that mimic real-world problems. The students in this study were told that free movie tickets would be given both to those whose group earned the most points in the social dilemma game, and to individuals who scored highest. Participants were then presented with the matrix in table 6.1, and asked to make five choices as to whether to cooperate or to get ahead.

The difficulty of the game is whether to make the choice to cooperate or to get ahead when you do not know what your peers are going to do. For example, if all four members of your group decide to cooperate, you will benefit (by getting 8 points) and your group will benefit (by getting 32 points, the maximum). However, you could individually earn more points if you chose to get ahead, but this would benefit you only if other members of your group chose to cooperate. That is, you would benefit by fooling your peers, and they would lose out due to your selfishness.

As expected, materialistic values were associated with more frequent decisions to get ahead rather than to cooperate. A less obvious finding was that materialistic students actually tended to gain fewer points in this social dilemma, in part because they tended to have friends with similar values. Consequently, they found themselves in groups composed of like-minded individuals whose values led them to care primarily about getting ahead rather than cooperating. As can be seen toward the bottom of the matrix in table 6.1, when many members of the group choose getting ahead, both individual scores and group scores decrease. In such cases, materialistic individuals "had no 'suckers' to exploit and could not trust each other to cooperate."[25] In a few cases, materialists did have others to exploit, however; five participants achieved the maximum possible individual score (55) by choosing to get ahead five times while their group-mates all cooperated each time. No surprise: those who took advantage of their peers' cooperation also scored rather high in materialistic values.

Summary

Materialistic values of wealth, status, and image work against close interpersonal relationships and connection to others, two hallmarks of psychological health and high quality of life. Several studies using samples of preschoolers, college students, and adults from all over the world reveal that valuing materialistic pursuits conflicts with valuing many characteristics of high-quality relationships as well as betterment of one's community and world. Thus, materialistic values lead people to "invest" less in their relationships and in their communities. Notably, this relative lack of care for connectedness is reflected in low-quality relationships characterized by little empathy and generosity, and by objectification, conflict, and feelings of alienation. Such values thus weaken the fibers that bind couples, friends, families, and communities together, thereby working against the satisfaction of our needs for intimacy and connection.

7

The Chains of Materialism

In the medieval system capital was the servant of man, but in the modern system it became his master.
—Erich Fromm[1]

We have thus far seen three ways in which materialistic values detract from our well-being: they maintain deep-rooted feelings of insecurity, they lead us to run on never-ending treadmills trying to prove our competence, and they interfere with our relationships. There remains to be explored one other way in which materialistic values work against our need satisfaction and psychological health: they diminish our personal freedom. Said differently, a strong focus on the pursuit of wealth, fame, and image undermines the satisfaction of needs for authenticity and autonomy.

But how can this be? Freedom and capitalism go hand in hand, and consumer goods and our appearance are two primary means by which we can express our individual identities. So we are told. But when my students in college insist that they are unique individuals who do whatever they want, I ask how many of them are wearing jeans at the moment. Generally it is about 75 percent of the class. Were I working in a corporation, the same would generally be true if I asked about gray suits and power ties. It is patently false that every consumer can "have it your way," for if every person truly expressed his or her identity through consumer goods, no company could survive; profit margins rely on mass production and mass consumption. Ads may try to convince us that we are unique because we own or desire a particular product, but we must always remember that they target thousands or millions of people. Ads are designed to sell prepackaged individualities.

If freedom is not really about the opportunity to choose from thousands of jeans designs, to decide which features we want on a car, or to pick a particular toothpaste, what exactly is it about? What does it mean to be who we really are and to feel autonomous and authentic?

To answer these questions, I draw on humanistic and existential theorizing, especially from models of human behavior developed by Edward Deci and Richard Ryan.[2] These thinkers agree that being autonomous:

means to act in accord with one's self—it means feeling free and volitional in one's actions. When autonomous, people are fully willing to do what they are doing, and they embrace the activity with a sense of interest and commitment. Their actions emanate from their true sense of self, so they are being authentic. In contrast, to be controlled means to act because one is being pressured. When controlled, people act without a sense of personal endorsement. Their behavior is not an expression of the self, for the self has been subjugated to the controls. In this condition, people can reasonably be described as alienated.[3]

To illustrate this definition, consider two people who go to church every Sunday. One of these people might do so autonomously, because the people she communes with, the songs she sings, and the prayers she recites all provide her with a deep sense of satisfaction. She finds being at church stimulating, interesting, and enjoyable, and she is strongly committed to it. It feels to her like a full expression of her truest desires, interests, and needs. The other person feels controlled and alienated when going to church. Although he still shows up every Sunday, his motivation is primarily to look good in the community. Furthermore, he knows his wife and in-laws would give him a hard time if he were to sleep in on Sundays. Finally, he has a lingering concern that God might punish him for his failures when he dies, so he hopes that attending church will provide a few points in his favor. His motivation is external rather than internal, and derives primarily from pressures and demands. Even though his body walks into church on Sundays, his real self does not.[4]

As we proceed through this chapter, I will continue to expand on the meanings of autonomy and authenticity. My main purpose, however, is not so much to develop new insights into these ideas, but to review empirical evidence indicating that materialistic values do a poor job of satisfying needs for authenticity and autonomy. First, we will see that people with a strong orientation to materialism tend to place less value on freedom and self-expression, and thus decrease their likelihood of having experiences characterized by these qualities. Second, focusing on materialistic rewards undermines experiences that some psychologists believe to be paragons of freedom and autonomy. Finally, strongly materialistic people often feel controlled and alienated in several aspects of their lives, and thus their needs for autonomy and authenticity are relatively poorly satisfied.

Valuing Freedom

The previous chapter showed that individuals who are strongly oriented toward materialistic values place little emphasis on valuing connectedness to others and the community; it is difficult to impress others and simultaneously be warmly connected with them. A similar value conflict is evident between materialism and autonomy. To the extent that people value wealth, fame, and image, they correspondingly place less value on authenticity and freedom.

Across the thousands of people who have filled out the Aspiration Index, results consistently show that individuals who strongly value materialistic, extrinsic aspirations place relatively less value on aspirations such as, "I will choose what I do, instead of being pushed along by life," "I will follow my interests and curiosity where they take me," and "I will feel free." Similarly, Patricia and Jacob Cohen found that teenagers for whom fame and looks are a high priority report less concern with being "myself no matter what" and understanding "myself." Ronald Inglehart's cross-cultural work on social values leads to a similar conclusion: materialistic values contrast with freedom-oriented values such as, "more say in government decisions," and "protect freedom of speech."[5]

The cross-cultural work of Shalom Schwartz also yields results documenting this value conflict. The circumplex model of value systems described in chapter 6 not only shows that materialistic values contradict those for benevolence and universalism, but those for self-direction as well.[6] Self-direction values are defined as reflecting "independent thought and action—choosing, creating, exploring." They involve concerns for choosing one's own goals, freedom, and creativity, as well as being curious and independent.

My understanding of the conflict between materialism and autonomy is that they represent two fundamentally different motivational systems that are responsible for driving behavior. Materialism derives from a motivational system focused on rewards and praise; autonomy and self-expression derive from a motivational system concerned with expression of interest, enjoyment, and challenge, and of doing things for their own sake. As described in the next section, substantial experimental evidence documents the antithetical nature of these two orientations to behavior and life.

Materialism, Intrinsic Motivation, and Flow

Throughout this book I have suggested that values lead people to seek and react to certain experiences in particular ways. If individuals place a low value on freedom and self-expression, they will be unlikely to construct their lives in a manner that enhances their chances of having autonomous and authentic experiences. Furthermore, values influence how people interpret experiences that just happen to occur. Two people with different values who are in the exact same situation are going to look for (and find) different things in that situation, and thus construct their experiences in different ways. As discussed earlier with regard to relationships, values bleed over into people's experiences, enhancing or detracting from them.

One experience from which materialistic values detract is the sort that some thinkers consider the pinnacle of autonomy and self-expression. Such an experience is called "intrinsically motivated" by Deci and Ryan, while Mihalyi Csikszentmihalyi labels it "flow."[7] Regardless of the name, it occurs when an individual is doing something for no other purpose than the sheer joy, interest, and challenge involved. A great example of intrinsic motivation is children's play, but it can also be seen in any number of adult activities, such as climbing mountains, painting pictures, hiking in the woods, and even writing books. People can also feel flow or intrinsic motivation in nonleisure activities, such as their work or conversations they have with others. What is required is that people pursue activities for what the activities themselves have to offer, not for rewards or praise. In the midst of such experiences, people often report a sense of strong connection and oneness with whatever they are doing. Often, they become so deeply involved in the activity that they almost forget about themselves. Perhaps as a result, after a flow experience, they often find that much more time has passed than they would have imagined.

During these experiences people feel most themselves, as though their behavior emanates from their authentic interests and needs. They feel free and fully behind what they are doing. As such, frequent flow experiences are important ways to satisfy our needs for authenticity and autonomy.

At least three aspects of a materialistic value orientation work against intrinsically motivated experiences, and therefore against satisfying these needs. First, it leads individuals to become more focused on external rewards that might be gained by activities than on interest, challenge, and flow. This undermines intrinsic motivation, and thus autonomy and agency. Materialistic values can also lead individuals to become especially self-conscious about how others see them. As a result, intrinsically motivated experiences are diminished, as they require losing awareness of oneself. Finally, some behaviors that materialistic values encourage, such as watching television, rarely have characteristics of flow. Thus, people with these values may spend much of their time in activities unlikely to satisfy their needs for autonomy and authenticity.

How Rewards Undermine Intrinsic Motivation

As stated, when we are intrinsically motivated, we do what we do because it is enjoyable, involving, and challenging. One of the most interesting questions researchers have asked about such experiences concerns what happens when people are rewarded for doing the things they find intrinsically motivating. If rewards are important motivators of behavior, giving people money or praise for doing something they enjoy could increase their motivation. On the other hand, it could lead people to care more about the rewards than the activity, and consequently to experience less interest and enjoyment. As such, rewards might decrease intrinsic motivation.

Edward Deci addressed this issue in 1971 by conducting an experiment in which students played with SOMA puzzles, three-dimensional cubes that can be made into various geometric structures.[8] Most people find that playing with SOMA cubes is an interesting and challenging activity that they would do just for the fun of it. All the students played with the puzzles, but whereas some received no external reward, others were paid a small amount of money. Later, once the participants thought the study was over, Deci surreptitiously watched how long participants played with the puzzles when they also had other things they could do, such as read magazines. Subjects who had been paid spent less time playing with the puzzles when they had other options. The reward apparently decreased participants' motivation for the activity they had originally found fun.

Since this study, dozens more like it have been conducted, with children and adults, with various types of rewards, and across school, work, and sports settings. Indeed, a powerful and extensive meta-analysis statistically summarized the results of 128 studies examining whether rewards undermine intrinsic motivation, and provided strong evidence that rewards do decrease people's motivation, interest, and enjoyment for what are initially intrinsically motivating activities.[9] Deci and Ryan believe that rewards undermine intrinsic motivation because they change people's focus about why they are doing something. When initially engaged in something enjoyable, people are motivated by a sense of choice and freedom. If you ask them why they are playing with SOMA puzzles, for instance, they would probably reply, "Because I choose to," "Because I like it," or "Because it is fun." After they are rewarded, however, people's sense of the cause of their behavior shifts from internal to external, and now they might reply, "For the money," or "To show how good I am at it."

Materialistic values lead people to enter into activities focused on rewards. As a consequence, those who believe in the importance of such pursuits are unlikely to experience the deeper internal satisfactions that occur when they are intrinsically motivated. Their concern with money and praise distracts them from the interesting, enjoyable, and challenging aspects of what they are doing.

Shivani Khanna and I tested this idea by measuring the materialistic value orientation of Indian and United States college students.[10] Students also completed a questionnaire that measures whether people are more intrinsically or extrinsically motivated in their work activities.[11] Intrinsically motivated people agree with statements conveying a sense of challenge and enjoyment in their activities, such as, "The more difficult the problem, the more I enjoy trying to solve it," and "I want my work to provide me with opportunities for increasing my knowledge and skills." Extrinsically oriented individuals, on the other hand, tend to agree with statements showing a focus on compensation and other rewards, such as, "I'm less concerned with what work I do than what I get for it," and "I am strongly motivated by the grades I can earn." Both Indian and United States students who were highly focused on materialistic values reported less intrinsic and more extrinsic motivation for their school work.

A second element of this study further indicated that a materialistic value orientation works against flow and intrinsic motivation. All participants wrote down the two work and leisure activities they spent the most time doing and the two people with whom they spent the most time. Next, they rated these six activities on seven dimensions relevant to experiences of alienation on the one hand and autonomy on the other. For example, participants reported how much they were bored versus challenged, trapped versus free, and alienated versus engaged in these activities. Highly materialistic Indian students reported that their work activities had fewer characteristics of flow and more of alienation. In addition, United States students reported the same regarding their leisure activities and their relationships with others.

Another good example of the way in which materialistic desires undermine positive experiences comes from research with four groups of college students from the United States and South Korea.[12] Ken Sheldon and his colleagues asked them to describe the most satisfying event they had in the preceding week, month, or semester and then rate how much they felt pleasant (happy, proud) and unpleasant (sad, anxious) emotions during the event. Finally, they rated how much these events were characterized by feelings of close connections to others, freedom and choice, self-esteem, and so on. One other characteristic they were asked about was the extent to which money, popularity, and luxury were salient during the satisfying event. When money or luxury was important, people's emotions were less positive and more negative. Said differently, students were least satisfied when they were focused on those features as crucial components of the event.

These results suggest that in their day-to-day experience, people with strong materialistic values focus on rewards rather than fun, interest, and challenge. This is notable in their work, relationships, and leisure activities. Such an attitude sabotages feelings of flow and intrinsic motivation, as people have fewer experiences conducive to the free expression of their own interests and thus less fulfillment of their needs for autonomy and authenticity.

Public Self-Consciousness
Recall that one prerequisite for the experience of flow and intrinsic motivation is being completely engaged in an activity. Consider, for example, those times when you are having fun doing something, be it dancing, speaking to others, or whatever, when suddenly you become quite aware of yourself. When this happens, the flow typically ends. I experience this sometimes when I am playing the piano. At first, I will just be enjoying playing or singing, and then I become more focused on myself than on the music. When this happens, I find that I play worse and do not enjoy myself nearly as much.

When people become highly focused on themselves, they experience what psychologists call "public self-consciousness," or a strong concern with how they appear to others. Although recognizing that other people have opinions and feelings about us is useful and adaptive, the bulk of the research finds that such self-focus is usually rather unpleasant. Typically, when we are publicly self-conscious, we focus on some personal fault or inadequacy, feel foolish or silly for something we have done, or feel incompetent. In addition, people who report frequent occurrences of public self-consciousness report high frequencies of depression, neuroticism, and narcissism.[13]

When people become too concerned with what others think of them, they become less focused on the challenges and enjoyment inherent in the fun activities they are doing. In support of this idea, Ryan and his colleagues have conducted experiments in which participants did intrinsically motivated activities, such as playing with SOMA puzzles, while being monitored by other people or by video cameras. Cameras and other people made them especially concerned with how they looked to others; it is no surprise, then, that such surveillance undermines intrinsic motivation.[14]

Evidence has been presented earlier suggesting that people with a strong orientation to materialism frequently feel self-conscious. First, they highly value recognition and status, which by definition involve a concern with others' opinions. Second, their self-esteem requires frequent bolstering by the praise of others. Support for this also comes from research by Jonathan Schroeder and Sanjiv Dugal, who administered Belk's materialism scale to a sample of college students in California.[15] Participants also completed a survey measuring their level of public self-consciousness. High public self-consciousness is indicated on this scale by agreement with items such as, "I'm concerned about what other people think of me," "I usually worry about making a good impression," and "I'm self-conscious about the way I look." As predicted, students scoring high on Belk's measure of materialism also reported frequent experiences of public self-consciousness.

These data support the second explanation for why needs for autonomy are poorly satisfied in people with a strong materialistic value orientation. Because materialistic values heighten concern with how others view us, and because they hamper experiences of flow and intrinsic motivation, they work against freedom and autonomy.

Materialism and Low-Flow Activities

There is one last and rather tantalizing explanation for why materialistic values and intrinsically motivated experiences are negatively associated, although more data have to be collected. Some evidence suggests that the behaviors and experiences encouraged by materialistic values are typically rather low in potential flow. As such, people with these values may spend much of their daily life engaged in relatively unsatisfying activities.

One example of low-flow behavior encouraged by materialistic values is watching television. Studies by Mihalyi Csikszentmihalyi and his colleagues have found that watching television involves very little challenge; instead, it causes people to feel zoned out or apathetic. Antonella Delle Fave has provided more evidence for this conclusion. When participants (who included Italian adolescents and textile craftsmen) were asked about the types of activities that brought them feelings of flow, watching television was rarely mentioned.[16]

Shopping is another example of a low-flow activity encouraged by materialistic values. To obtain the possessions that enhance their materialistic aspirations, people must generally shop. But again, Delle Fave's research shows that people rarely mentioned purchasing things as an activity that provided flow.[17] Given the stresses and hassles involved in shopping, and the fact that the focus on money and rewards is likely to undermine intrinsic motivation, such a low occurrence of flow should not be surprising.

Working long hours and amassing debt are other activities encouraged by materialistic values that must surely involve little in the way of intrinsic satisfaction. As noted by Juliet Schor, contemporary United States culture leads many people to work a great deal of overtime and go deeply into debt in order to afford the lifestyle the culture says conveys success and happiness.[18] The price of overwork and debt is stress, which is fundamentally opposed to the freedom and autonomy characteristic of intrinsic motivation and flow.

Pressure and Coercion

The demands of life are such that all of us, regardless of our materialistic aspirations, have fewer experiences of flow on a daily basis than we might like. For many of us, our routine consists less frequently of climbing mountains and having moments of deep interest at work than of taking out the garbage and engaging in rote tasks. But even though these latter activities only rarely provide intrinsic motivation, we can still feel more or less autonomous and authentic or controlled and alienated while we are doing them. Put differently, we can take out the trash because we really value a clean, hygienic house, or because we feel pressured by our spouse or our conscience.

Our freedom and agency can thus be understood as relative. In all activities and spheres of life, we can feel more or less authentic in what we are doing, why we are doing it, and how we are doing it. To represent this continuum of autonomy, table 7.1 shows different reasons or motivations people sometimes give for their behavior.[19] As elucidated by Ryan and

Table 7.1
Autonomy and reasons for behaving—from Ryan (1995)

Regulation/ Reason	Intrinsic	Identified	Introjected	External
Relative autonomy	Very high	High	Low	Very low
Self-causation	Internal	Internal	External	External
Associated processes	Interest Enjoyment Challenge Flow	Conscious valuing Commitment Acceptance	Guilt Anxiety-avoidance Self-esteem maintenance	Compliance Reward pursuit Punishment avoidance

Reprinted by permission of Blackwell Publishers.

Deci, each motivation entails a related set of feelings and psychic processes that make people feel more or less free, and each is more or less expressive of people's true selves.

The first two reasons on the continuum are intrinsic and identified, which represent relatively high levels of autonomy and self-causation. As noted, when individuals do things because of intrinsic reasons, they are motivated by interest, enjoyment, and challenge. In such instances they feel free and autonomous because they themselves are the true source of their behavior. People also feel free and autonomous if they identify with what they are doing. When people have reflected deeply on their goals or behavior and believe that a particular course of action is in line with their commitments and values, they experience freedom and autonomy. For example, even though I may not find changing my son's diaper to be challenging and enjoyable, I feel autonomous when I do it because I believe it is important for his health and comfort, and for my commitment to him as his father.

In contrast to autonomous motivations, people sometimes feel pressured in their behaviors. As shown in table 7.1, they are externally motivated when they do something to gain rewards and praise or to avoid censure. In such cases, they do not own their behavior, but instead act from a sense of being controlled or coerced. Similarly, people sometimes are motivated by "introjects," which involve internal pressure. When they do something because they would feel bad about themselves if they did not do it, or to maintain their perhaps contingent self-esteem, their behavior is driven by compulsion and coercion rather than by freedom and authenticity. Think back to the man who went to church just to look good to his community, to avoid the reprobation of his family, and to please God. These are examples of introjected and external motives.

Several lines of evidence converge to show that people with a strong materialistic value orientation frequently report motivations from the controlled, nonautonomous end of the continuum. In several samples of United States college students and adults, Ken Sheldon and I have consistently discovered that those who strive toward materialistic outcomes often report that they pursue their goals because they believe they ought to, because they would feel ashamed, guilty, or anxious if they didn't, because someone else wants them to, because the situation compels it, or because they will obtain rewards or avoid punishment.[20] Such motivations reflect pressure and coercion, and thus work against satisfaction of needs for autonomy and authenticity.

Even in arenas of life such as having possessions, making money, and shopping, where we might expect people with a strong materialistic value orientation to feel relatively free, problems in autonomy and authenticity are nonetheless present. For example, Marsha Richins asked adults high and low in materialism to "list your most important possessions and explain why each is important to you." Highly materialistic individuals listed more reasons concerning appearance and the monetary worth of the items (external and introjected regulation) and fewer reasons concerning enjoyment (intrinsic reasons).[21] Similarly, Abhishek Srivastava and his colleagues presented 266 business students and 145 entrepreneurs with a list of different motives for making money, including reasons such as feeling secure, pursuing leisure activities, and donating money to those who need it.[22] Participants were also asked how important financial success was in comparison to other goals. Across both samples, the only types of motives consistently related to placing a strong value on materialism were social comparison (e.g., "To have a house and cars that are better than those of my neighbors") and overcoming self-doubt (e.g., "To prove that I am not as dumb as some people assumed"). In other words, although these business students and entrepreneurs could report many types of reasons for pursuing financial success, those with strong materialistic values were typically most concerned with appearing successful to others and maintaining their sense of self-esteem. As shown in table 7.1, both of these types of motives poorly satisfy autonomy needs. It is also important to note that Srivastava found that much of the statistical association between materialistic values and low well-being could be accounted for by these controlled, nonautonomous motives. This suggests that, at least for those in business, poor satisfaction of autonomy needs may be one of the most important explanations why highly materialistic individuals are less happy.

Shopping is another materialistic behavior in which compulsion and pressure are often evident. Consumer researchers and psychiatrists have investigated "compulsive buying," a psychopathology characterized by intense impulses to purchase things even when people know that they do not need the items.[23] One compulsive buyer in a study by Ronald Faber and Thomas O'Guinn reported, "It was like I was on automatic" when shopping. Another said, "It's not that I want it, because sometimes, I'll just buy it and I'll think, 'Ugh, another sweatshirt.'" A third stated, "I can never go even to the [grocery store] and buy one quart of milk. I've always got to buy two."

These examples show that compulsive buyers do not believe that they choose to purchase these products; instead, they experience mounting pressure or anxiety that can seemingly be relieved only by buying. Other compulsive buyers are driven by a hope that they will be liked and well treated by shopkeepers (contingent self-esteem). For example, two participants in O'Guinn and Faber's studies reported how much they reveled in the special attention they received from sales personnel and from UPS drivers who delivered their packages. One went so far as to say, "I thought I was pleasing the store" when buying.

The facts that compulsive buyers have an overwhelming and uncontrollable desire to purchase, are driven to purchase so they can avoid feelings of anxiety, and often try to obtain others' approval are consistent with the idea that they are acting from introjected or extrinsic motivation. That is, when compelled to purchase, they feel pressure akin to addiction. Even though buying seems to derive from nonautonomous motivations, they nonetheless persist as a means of maintaining their contingent

Table 7.2
Sample items from Faber and O'Guinn's (1992) clinical screener for compulsive buying

---

If I have any money left at the end of the pay period, I just have to spend it.
I have bought things even though I couldn't afford them.
I have bought myself something in order to make myself feel better.
I have felt anxious or nervous on days when I didn't go shopping.

Reprinted by permission of the University of Chicago Press.

self-esteem and avoiding anxiety. As with all addictive behaviors, needs for authenticity and autonomy are undermined, as is personal well-being.

Not all people with strong materialistic values are compulsive buyers, but many adults who score high on the screening instrument for compulsive buying presented in table 7.2 also score high on measures of materialism. In addition, compulsive buyers have relatively low self-esteem and higher rates of depression, anxiety disorders, and substance use disorders, compared with normal shoppers. As shown earlier, these problems also characterize people who believe in the importance of materialistic values.

Summary

This chapter discusses many ways in which an orientation to materialistic values works against authenticity and autonomy. Materialistic values are associated with placing little value on freedom and self-direction, thereby decreasing the likelihood of satisfying these needs. Individuals strongly concerned with materialistic values also enter experiences already focused on obtaining rewards and praise, rather than on enjoying the challenges and inherent pleasures of activities. As such, they miss out on experiences of autonomy and authenticity. Furthermore, their values direct them toward activities such as watching television and shopping that rarely provide flow or intrinsic motivation. Finally, materialistic values are associated with a tendency to feel pressured and compelled, even in behaviors consistent with these values. All of this suggests that, rather than providing paths to freedom and autonomy, people feel chained, pressured, and controlled when they focus on materialistic values.

8

Family, Community, and the Earth

The insolence of wealth will creep out.
—Samuel Johnson[1]

The thrust of the book thus far has been on some of the internal, personal consequences of embracing materialistic values. I have explored how our experiences change, how our needs remain unfulfilled, and how our well-being declines when materialistic values become central to what we believe is important in life. In addition, these values have a host of external consequences. Our lovers, our children, our neighbors, our society, and our planet are all affected when the desire for wealth, status, and image directs our behavior. In this chapter I revisit some research presented earlier and present new evidence to describe how materialistic values harm those around us, as well as how they damage the health of our planet.

Marriage

Imagine that you are married to a person who is strongly committed to materialistic values. On the basis of research reviewed in chapter 6, we can expect that your spouse may not care as much as you might hope about expressing his or her appreciation for you, about helping you, or about being loyal, responsible, honest, and forgiving. In addition your spouse is probably not especially inclined to try to understand your point of view or to be very generous. When conflicts occur, your spouse may be somewhat aggressive, manipulative, and distrustful. Finally, you might have the sense that your spouse is using you to help bolster his or her self-esteem or to get ahead in life.

Such behaviors and attitudes work against your spouse's subjective well-being, as they create experiences that fail to satisfy her or his needs for intimacy and connection. But these values also influence you by producing an interpersonal environment that frustrates satisfaction of your needs. Being devalued and treated in an objectified manner does little to fulfill your needs and thus decreases the quality of your life.

An outside observer looking in on such a marriage would probably predict its eventual dissolution. Clearly divorce is complexly determined, but might it be that materialistic values have a role? The facts that divorce rates are quite high in consumer cultures and have increased as our society has become more materialistic are consistent with this supposition. So is the fact that disagreements about money are reported by spouses to be a major source of conflict in marriage.[2]

Research must be conducted on how materialistic values affect marriage, but it seems likely that spouses highly focused on making money and buying things that signify the "good life" find little quality time to share with each other. Furthermore, when hard times come, as they always will in a relationship, fewer commonalities and less empathy may exist to connect spouses and help them find solutions to their problems. Finally, I would predict that when people's love relationships are based on enhancing their own status, rather than on mutuality, both individuals are unlikely to feel appreciated for who they really are.

Parenting

Materialistic values are also implicated in our roles as parents. When they guide our behavior, our children watch and soak it up. Evidence suggests that children's value systems develop in part through imitation of what their parents value,[3] whether that be materialism or otherwise. In our study of the heterogeneous sample of teens mentioned earlier, my colleagues and I found a significant association between the values of mothers and children.[4] Of seventy mothers who rated financial success values as relatively important compared with self-acceptance values, fifty of their teens (71%) responded the same. Conversely, of fifty-nine mothers who preferred self-acceptance to financial success, thirty-seven of their teens

(63%) did so as well. Similar results were found when comparing financial success with affiliation and community values.

Transmission of materialistic values from parent to child involves more than a parent holding such values; it also depends on specific parent behaviors that encourage and reinforce these values in their children. For example, I would expect that parents with materialistic values would watch substantial amounts of television. As a result, their children are probably exposed to a large number of messages that reinforce these values. The fact that such values are associated with less empathic and more conflictual relationships suggests that they might lead parents to be less nurturing with their children. In the study of mothers and teens, mothers with materialistic aspirations were not especially nurturing, which is a parenting style associated with high materialistic values in teens (see chapter 4).[5]

Other behaviors driven by materialistic values can send an implicit message to children that wealth and status are of primary importance. To the extent we work long hours to maintain a materialistic lifestyle, we spend less time with our children. I am not talking here about the many people who must work two jobs to feed, clothe, and shelter their families. I refer to those of us who work long hours to fulfill less basic needs, such as two new minivans in the garage of our 2,500-square-foot house. When children see such behavior, they also see that work, money, and possessions are of great importance, perhaps of more importance than family.

Many parents I speak with feel guilty about the long hours they work and the impact this has on their children. Unfortunately, the way that they sometimes compensate only adds fuel to the materialistic fire: they express their love and assuage their guilt by buying gifts for their kids. Video games and stylish sneakers can never replace hugs and time spent together, however. What's more, such purchases have the added effects of allowing material goods to infiltrate the relationships with children and of reinforcing the consumer message that love is truest when money is spent.

The upshot, of course, is that when parenting is influenced by materialistic values, children are increasingly likely to value wealth and possessions highly. The consequences of this have been made clear.

Community

In today's interconnected world, communities are no longer limited by geographical boundaries. Our community includes people we interact with on the Internet, multinational corporations who sell us things, celebrities populating the media, and politicians whose decisions affect our lives. Like everyone else, the actions of these people reflect their values. When powerful people hold strong material values, the whole of society bears some of the costs.

Research reviewed earlier showed that materialistic values are associated with making more antisocial and self-centered decisions involving getting ahead rather than cooperating. As a result, others in the community are treated as objects to be manipulated and used. Materialistic values also conflict with concern for making the world a better place, and the desire to contribute to equality, justice, and other aspects of civil society.

Consider, for example, how materialistic values influence business executives' decisions regarding the workforce of their companies. Such choices often involve a clear value conflict: do I make more money for myself and the shareholders who gave me a job, or should I treat workers' needs as equal to those of shareholders? In business decisions, materialistic values often win out, as was the case when Lee Iacocca cut merit pay for Chrysler employees but took a $20 million bonus for himself. His comment afterward? "That's the American way. If little kids don't aspire to make money like I did, what the hell good is this country?"[6]

The effects on the community are also clear when government officials create (or rescind) laws and tax structures that underfund health, education, environment, and art programs but allow multinational corporations to have greater financial assets and power than some nations. The choice is a clear one for money over social equality, nature, and aesthetics.

I could continue enumerating the manifold ways in which materialistic values influence doctors and medical care, athletes and sports, teachers and education, or almost any other realm of social life. Rather than restate what many before me have said quite well,[7] I will finish this section by discussing some members of our community who are extremely powerful, but at the same time quite invisible.

It is easy to forget that advertisements are designed by people, as marketers and advertisers rarely become celebrities and credits almost never roll after a commercial. Nonetheless, we must always remember that someone chose to make an ad that is selling a particular product and propagating consumer mindsets. Those men and women have great power, as their work is seen almost everywhere and influences a large segment of society.

With this in mind, read the following quotations about how some people who design and pay for ads think about marketing their wares to children:[8]

There are only two ways to increase customers. Either you switch them to your brand or you grow them from birth.

—James U. McNeal, professor of marketing at Texas A&M

All of these people understand something that is very basic and logical, that if you own this child at an early age, you can own this child for years to come. Companies are saying, "Hey, I want to own the kid younger and younger and younger."

—Mike Searles, president of Kids 'R' Us, a chain of children's specialty stores

When it comes to targeting kid consumers, we at General Mills follow the Procter & Gamble model of "cradle to grave." We believe in getting them early and having them for life.

—Wayne Chilicki, executive at General Mills

Advertising at its best is making people feel that without their product, you're a loser. Kids are very sensitive to that . . . You open up emotional vulnerabilities, and it's very easy to do with kids because they're the most emotionally vulnerable.

—Nancy Shalek, president of the Shalek Agency

Consider the words used by these people. Children are grown, owned, targeted, "had," and intentionally made to feel emotionally vulnerable. They are understood as little consumers whose money can be taken from them by the right ad as easily as candy could be taken from them only a few years earlier. From the perspective of some marketers and advertisers, children are objects who may be profitably manipulated in order to make money.

When materialistic values dominate our society, we move farther and farther from what makes us civilized. We treat each other in less humane ways. We allow the pursuit of money to take precedence over equality, the human spirit, and respectful treatment of each other. We permit materialistic values to undermine much of what could be the very best about our communities.

The Earth

Many scientists believe that overconsumption is one of the fundamental problems threatening the well-being and integrity of Earth's ecosystem.[9] Humans, particularly in the Western Hemisphere, are consuming resources at a pace that far outweighs Earth's ability both to renew these resources and absorb the resultant wastes. Water, forests, and clean air are all being used and polluted at rates far higher than those at which they are being replaced, and wastes resulting from consumption and production are believed by many scientists to be causing holes in the ozone layer, among a litany of other problems. Biodiversity has been shrinking as habitats of animals and plants are destroyed or turned into small islands of park, separated from each other by "development." Such problems have led many scientists and environmentalists to worry greatly over the health of our planet's ecosystem and its ability to support life.

The forces at work threatening Earth's well-being are tremendous and complex, and I do not wish to reduce them solely to a value question. Yet we must recognize the place of materialism in the equation, as substantial evidence shows that choices arising from a materialistic value orientation are often unconcerned with, or actively hostile toward, nature.

We have seen instances of how materialistic values conflict with concern for the wider world. For example, individuals focused on materialistic values care less about "beautiful cities and countryside."[10] Similarly, the circumplex model of values shows that across many cultures, values for wealth oppose concerns to "protect the environment," to have a "world of beauty," and to attain "unity with nature."[11]

Other evidence exists that materialistic values are associated with low interest in environmental and ecological issues. Shaun Saunders and Dan Munro showed that Australians who strongly expressed materialistic values also reported negative attitudes toward the environment, little love of all living things, and few ecologically friendly behaviors.[12] Marsha Richins and Scott Dawson's study of the materialism of over 200 adults in the United States yielded similar results.[13] Participants completed a survey asking how often they engaged in three types of ecologically healthy practices: those that are materially simple (riding a bike instead of driving a car, buying used instead of new products), those that involve more self-determination (making one's own bread rather than buying it, doing home repairs oneself), and those evidencing greater ecological awareness (recycling and contributing to environmental organizations). People with strong materialistic values scored lower on each of these measures, and thus engaged in more ecologically damaging behaviors.

The ultimate problem implied by these studies is that if we continue to be driven by selfishness and materialism, ecological disaster awaits us. Years of social dilemma research shows that human behaviors frequently bring about such problems, a process sometimes called "the tragedy of the commons."[14] Consider, for example, a community pasture that a number of individuals share. As long as all the shepherds limit the number of sheep that graze, the pasture will remain in good shape and provide enough food for everyone's sheep, because the grass, clover, and other plants grow back quickly. What often occurs, however, is that one individual will add more and more sheep to his herd, thus using more of the common resource. As the pasture becomes increasingly spare from overgrazing, other individuals also add more sheep. Soon, of course, the entire resource is gone, and no one can graze their sheep there any longer.

Ken Sheldon and Holly McGregor recognized that materialistic values are likely to lead individuals to make the environmental and competitive choices that cause the tragedy of the commons.[15] To test this idea, the Aspiration Index was administered to over 150 students at the University of Rochester. Based on their scores, students were classified as high or low in materialistic values and then placed in one of three groups: four materialistic people, two materialistic and two nonmaterialistic people, or four nonmaterialistic people. Groups engaged in an extended version of the forest-management game (described in chapter 4) and were asked to imagine that they were the head of a timber company that, along with three other companies, was logging in the same 200-hectare (1 hectare = 100 acres) national forest. Each year, each company could bid to cut up to 1,000 acres of the forest; thus the forest might shrink by as much as 4,000 acres every year, although whatever remained would

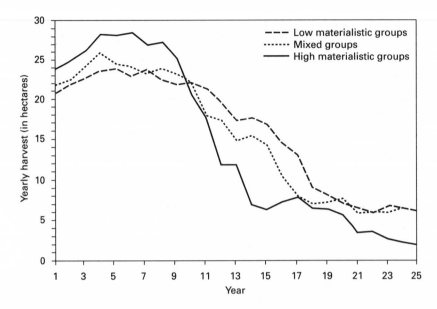

Figure 8.1
Yearly harvest in hectares of three groups of students differing in their value orientations. (Modified from Sheldon and McGregor, 2000. Reprinted by permission of Blackwell Publishers.)

grow back at a rate of 10 percent a year. All participants were reminded that if they bid to harvest only a few acres, their company might not profit much, whereas if they bid to harvest many acres, the forest might be decimated. Each participant in the group then made a bid for the first year's harvest; a research assistant recorded the bids and calculated how many acres remained (after adding in the 10 percent growth) for the next year's bid. Bidding continued until the forest was gone or until twenty-five years had passed.

Figure 8.1 shows yearly harvests for the three groups across the twenty-five years. Materialistic groups initially harvested more than did the less materialistic groups. As a result, the amount of forest steeply declined, and materialistic groups were able to harvest less and less as time went on. In fact, over time, less materialistic groups actually made *more* profit than did materialistic groups, because their forests remained larger for a longer period of time. In addition, although the forests of less materialistic groups were preserved for almost twenty years on average, those of materialistic groups lasted only fifteen years on average.

The implications of this experiment are straightforward. When materialistic values drive our behavior, everyone loses, both humans and the other species who inhabit the "resource" and call it "home."

Summary

This chapter shows that materialistic values not only undermine the well-being of those who strongly hold them, but also negatively affect the health and happiness of many others. When interactions with people are based on such values, less empathy and intimacy are present in relationships, and materialistic values are more likely to be transmitted to the next generation. The broader community will also be damaged when those in power objectify others in their pursuit of wealth and status. Finally, Earth's health suffers as these values lead individuals to consume at unsustainable and damaging rates.

9

Making Change

Riches are not from abundance of worldly goods, but from a contented mind.
—Muhammad[1]

Throughout this book I have presented scientific data to show the truth
of Muhammad's statement: a life centered around making money and
attaining renown is not meaningful. We saw in chapter 2 that materialistic values go hand in hand with low quality of life and psychological
health. In chapters 4 through 7 we saw that needs for security and safety,
competence and self-esteem, connectedness to others, and autonomy and
authenticity are relatively unsatisfied when materialistic values are prominent in people's value systems. Chapter 8 described some of the ways
that materialistic values work against the well-being of other people, society, and the planet. From all of this the issue is clear: materialistic values
undermine our quality of life.

Now that we know the problem, two questions must be confronted.
First, we must ask what is an alternative vision of personal and social
life that is not centered on materialistic aims? Second, we must ask the
even more difficult question, how do we go about implementing the
changes necessary to reach a more inwardly rich vision of the good life?

In seeking answers I have found it helpful to continue framing the problem of materialism as one of values. On the one hand, people obtain their
values from families, peers, social institutions, and the media. On the
other hand, society is composed of people, and its functioning depends
on the values of those people. Thus, people believe in materialism because
society is so materialistic, and society is so materialistic because many
people believe that materialistic pursuits are a path to happiness.

Such a chicken-and-egg problem could be cause for despair, but I believe this interdependence is actually cause for hope. If we can change society, people's values will change, and if people decide to change, society's values will change. In essence, at least two broad inroads are available for implementing value shifts, should we individually and societally decide that is what we want.

This final chapter proposes an alternative vision to materialistic values and offers some strategies that might help decrease these values for people and society and thus increase our well-being.

Healthy Values, Healthy Society

The need-based theory that organized this book, as well as empirical research conducted by various investigators, provides a good set of beginning guidelines for knowing which values are healthiest for individuals and society to pursue. Succinctly stated, the healthiest values are those that best reflect and support the needs outlined in chapter 3. Ideally, our values direct us to have experiences that help us feel safe and secure, competent and worthy, connected to others, and authentic and free.

My colleagues and I have called values that fulfill these psychological needs intrinsic.[2] Intrinsic values are based in people's real psychological needs, support their growth and development, and are inherently satisfying to pursue. Our research has focused on three main intrinsic values: self-acceptance and personal growth; relatedness and intimacy; and community feeling and helpfulness. Table 9.1 shows some of the items from the Aspiration Index that are used to measure these values.

Many studies reviewed in earlier chapters examined not only how materialistic values relate to well-being, but also how intrinsic values relate to psychological health. Compared with materialistic people, those who believe intrinsic values are relatively important report enhanced happiness, greater psychological health,[3] better interpersonal relationships,[4] more contribution to the community,[5] and more concern for ecological issues.[6] These findings are substantiated by work of researchers using different value measures,[7] and by research conducted with various age[8] and cultural groups.[9] Evidence also shows that relatively high attainment of intrinsic goals benefits well-being,[10] in contrast to what we saw in chap-

Table 9.1
Sample intrinsic value items from Kasser and Ryan's (1996) Aspiration Index

---

Self-acceptance/Personal growth
I will choose what I do, instead of being pushed along by life.
I will follow my interests and curiosity where they take me.
Relatedness/Intimacy
I will express my love for special people.
I will have a committed, intimate relationship.
Community feeling/Helpfulness
The things I do will make other people's lives better.
I will help the world become a better place.

---

ter 5 for materialistic pursuits. Presumably, intrinsic values lead us to engage in behaviors and have experiences that satisfy our underlying psychological needs. As these needs are satisfied, our well-being increases.

Many thinkers in other fields have propounded the benefits of values such as growing as a person, knowing and accepting oneself, caring about family and friends, and helping the community and world be a better place. The importance of these values can also be recognized in a contemporary social movement called Voluntary Simplicity,[11] a growing trend for people to abandon the high-paying, high-stress lifestyle necessary to support high levels of consumption, and focus instead on personal growth, nurturing relationships, and helping others.

In sum, I believe we must, at all possible levels, encourage internalization of values for personal growth, close interpersonal relationships, and contribution to one's community. Notably, these are the values that research reviewed in chapters 6 and 7 has shown are generally opposed to materialistic values. Thus, if they become dominant in our personal and societal value systems, materialism should decline, our personal well-being should rise, and we might alleviate some of the interpersonal, societal, and ecological problems discussed in chapter 8.

Making Change

How might we go about transforming value systems? One suggestion is to make changes at as many levels as possible in order to break the current pattern: society encourages materialistic values, so we adopt them and pursue more and more materialistic aims; such pursuits do not improve our happiness, so we look to society for suggestions on how to be happier; society tells us to become even more materialistic, and on it goes. If we can break this cycle at several of its links and put in its place a more humane and satisfying pattern based on intrinsic values, positive changes will be likely to accrue.

I suggest below a series of strategies, most of which have the dual purpose of decreasing materialistic values and increasing intrinsic values, that might be implemented at personal, familial, and societal levels. Although these levels overlap to some extent, the benefit of working at them all is that changes at one are likely to radiate out to others. By no means do I view the suggestions as all-inclusive; my expertise is too limited to develop a comprehensive list. Success will be most likely to occur if creative people from all backgrounds join together to find and implement additional and better ways to remake our society.

Personal Change

As a psychologist I am well aware of the difficulty of changing as a person—it can be arduous and painful. Furthermore, suggesting how to make personal changes by enumerating strategies in a book can be little more than giving advice, which research shows is not the most effective way to facilitate change.

Nonetheless, I hope that by basing the suggestions that follow on cited research, they will have a solid grounding. I would add that when we encounter problems changing our values (which most of us surely will), we would do well to seek help, be it from friends, family, therapists, religious leaders, or whomever we trust. By talking out issues and ideas with another person who is striving to understand us, we will certainly make more progress than by going it alone.

That said, here are a few ideas for possible personal change.

1. *Contemplate the meaning of this research.*   If you have come to agree that materialistic values undermine well-being, that is a good first step toward change. Just as some individuals change their smoking, drinking, eating, and exercise patterns as a result of becoming aware of medical

research on physical health, data reviewed in this book may be convincing enough to lead some of us to change our lifestyles. Indeed, research suggests that being confronted with concrete information about the consequences and implications of their values can lead people to change both their values and the behaviors relevant to them.[12]

Keep in mind that I am not advocating vows of poverty; making some money and having some possessions are necessary in our world. Resources help people feel secure, and security is a basic need that must be satisfied. But beyond that, empirical evidence suggests that wealth does very little to improve well-being. The trick is to keep materialistic aims in balance with intrinsic aims, and always to have healthier aims dominant. It is the same idea as keeping the relative percentage of calories derived from sweets and fats lower than those from grains, fruits, and vegetables. A little bit of chocolate cake (materialism) will not hurt you too much, as long as most of your calories come from fresh produce and whole grains (intrinsic values).

2. *Look at what is scaring you.*   This is of course hard advice, as by nature we want to avoid what is anxiety provoking. But we have seen in this book that materialism increases to the extent that we grow up with nonnurturing parents, to the extent we fear death, and to the extent we question our self-worth. All of these are frightening, unpleasant things to contemplate about ourselves, but until they are confronted, worked through, and accepted, they will continue to drive our behavior.

Sometimes people ask me what I would recommend lottery winners do with their money. I always suggest using some of it for therapy. Granted, I am a psychologist with a bias toward the power of talking out issues with a trained professional. But if you sense that something is not quite right in life, and if you wonder whether materialistic values might be involved, I can think of no wiser financial investment than in self-knowledge. It is the path to freedom, at many levels. By sorting through painful past experiences, irrational beliefs, and unacknowledged fears, people can become free of these chains and find healthier ways of coping than making money and consuming things. Some therapists are beginning to recognize the problems associated with compulsive consumption, striving for wealth and acquisitions, and even becoming wealthy, and are developing treatments to help individuals handle these issues.[13]

3. *Get off the materialistic treadmill.* Chapter 5 showed that part of the problem of materialistic values is that once they are incorporated into our value systems, they become the ideal for which we strive and the measure by which we determine our competence and self-worth. As a result, we constantly measure ourselves against unrealistic or ever-rising yardsticks and are thus rarely satisfied with what we have attained.

One way to solve the problem is to recognize inherent dissatisfaction in the rat race. The next time you are feeling somewhat empty or down, you may find that you think to yourself, "Maybe if I just had that new . . . ," or "Maybe if I could just make more money. . . ," or "Maybe if my body were just different in this way . . ." These are signs of starting the walk on the treadmill. Ask yourself whether you have engaged in these materialistic activities before. Ask yourself whether they really improved the quality of your life. My guess is that you might initially have felt better if you got what you were after, but your life did not really change, and those nagging insecurities quickly returned. If this is so, ask, "Why should I keep doing something that hasn't worked to make me feel better in the long run? What could I do instead?" To the extent that you pick something that will really satisfy your needs (an intrinsic pursuit), you will be likely to fill your emptiness and improve your well-being. Later in this section I am more specific about alternatives to materialistically driven behaviors, but an important early step is to recognize how the cycle begins.

4. *Ask yourself why you really want the money, looks, or fame.* I noted in chapter 7 that sometimes people begin to look at materialistic things as ends in themselves. The truth is that money is good only for buying food, shelter, safety, and other necessities; it can never really buy self-esteem, love, or freedom. If what you are really after is feeling good about yourself, figure out more direct paths than making money, trying to become beautiful, or impressing people with your status.

As before, ask yourself whether materialistic values have actually worked for you, or whether they continue to perpetuate your problems instead. If you find it is the latter, try new, more direct ways to satisfy your needs. Take a good look at what your needs really are. Are you lonely? Feeling disconnected from your community? Looking for a more challenging or fulfilling job? Want more opportunities for self-expression? Once you identify your true psychological needs it will be easier to find clearer paths to meeting them.

5. *Rethink your relationships.* Being in a relationship can be the most satisfying way to spend one's time, but if your relationships are problematic, stop to wonder what has happened. Have you been putting the time, energy, and thought into them that you have been in money and image? Are they characterized by empathy, mutuality, and sharing? Or do you see signs of objectification detailed in chapter 6?

Sit down and discuss these issues with your partner, with your friends, and with your family. Try to talk out your dissatisfactions with the way things are and see whether there might be more satisfying ways to interact with one another. Find ways to be with your partner that are focused more on the two of you than on materialism—go for a walk, talk about your interests, develop common hobbies. Spend time together, not just money on each other.

6. *Change your activities.* Although the things we do are partly rooted in our values, we can nonetheless change our behaviors before we change our values. We have free will, and we can decide we no longer want to watch six hours of television a day. We can remove activities from our lives that are low flow or that reinforce materialistic values and decrease self-esteem. Put the television in the closet. Cancel your subscription to glamour and gossip magazines. Stop wandering in the mall or shopping on the Internet. Try to take these activities out of your life for a month and observe what happens.

Chances are that at first you may not know what to do with yourself, and you might feel increasingly anxious and empty. The temptation will be to return to the old habits. It is just like someone who is trying to quit smoking—anxiety and the temptation to light up build and build. Rather than giving in, realize that now is the perfect time to form new habits. Go for a walk. Read a book. Do volunteer work. Meditate. Play with your children. Talk with your spouse. Go dancing. Shoot baskets. Work in a garden. Cook. Paint a picture. Play a musical instrument. Go fishing. Activities that are most satisfying will be those that are congruent with intrinsic values, those to which you feel drawn by your individuality. What will be most exciting and growth-producing for you cannot be mass produced and sold; you must find it yourself.

By engaging in new, intrinsically oriented behaviors, two important things are likely to happen. First, you will have more experiences that satisfy your needs. Thus, your happiness and well-being should rise. Second, by having such experiences, you will probably begin to see the value of intrinsic pursuits. As such, the healthier part of your value system will be strengthened, and the importance of materialism should begin to wane.

After having pursued intrinsically oriented behaviors for a month or so, stop and examine your life. Are you more satisfied now? Are you happier? Does life seem more meaningful? You know what I believe the answer will be, but the real test is what you find for yourself.

Family Change

Another route to change is to examine the processes by which our children are socialized into a consumer identity. In the same way that children are taught to have good manners, to behave like good boys and girls, not to fight, and so on, they are socialized to believe in the worth of materialistic pursuits and to think of themselves as wage earners and consumers. To endure, a capitalistic consumer society requires workers to make products that are sold so that the workers (and entrepreneurs who pay them) can have money to buy things other workers produce. Society is designed to inculcate materialistic values in our children, for if the next generation does not come to care about possessions, image, and status, we fear our economic and cultural systems will collapse.

Society works through various means to indoctrinate children, including the school system, behavior of parents, mass media, and the Internet. As the world has become increasingly materialistic, so have our children. Since the mid 1960s, Alexander Astin and his colleagues have been asking over 200,000 first-year college students in the United States what is important to them in life. The percentage of students who believe that it is very important or essential to "develop a meaningful philosophy of life" decreased from over 80 percent in the late 1960s to around 40 percent in the late 1990s. At the same time, the percentage who believe that it is very important or essential to "be very well off financially" has risen from just over 40 percent to over 70 percent.[14] Society's value-making machine is an effective one.

How can parents stem this tide?

1. *Remember the saying, "Monkey see, monkey do."* As discussed in chapter 8, when parents' behaviors reflect materialistic values, their children are likely to imitate them. When parents primarily express their love through things, children receive the message that love means things. When parents focus more on making money and attaining high status than on being with their family, their children will believe that materialistic aims are more important than the family or themselves.

As parents, we must take a long look at ourselves and recognize that we act as one of the socializing agents of materialistic culture. If we are displeased with this, we can change. Consider some of the suggestions above for ways to change your values to more healthy intrinsic ones. These behaviors will become what your children see at home, and what they will be likely to imitate.

2. *Change children's activities.* Although it is of great importance to limit our own exposure to materialistic messages, limiting children's exposure is all the more crucial. Common knowledge tells us to turn off the primary source of consumeristic propaganda, the television. Supporting this, the American Academy of Pediatrics recommends that children under two years of age view no television at all and that electronic media be removed from children's bedrooms.[15] Other effective ways of limiting materialistic messages include making tapes of programs that do not promote materialistic values and activating the mute button on the remote control during commercials. Send a message to your children that what is on television is not worthy of imitation.

We must look beyond television, however. Consider the magazines children read. Do they have articles about nature and family, or about looks, weight, and buying things? Consider the Internet. Look at Web sites your children visit and the underlying materialistic messages they send. Just as you might watch television with your children, surf the Web with them. Help them to understand what they see and to recognize the number of ads they encounter. Tell them that free Websites for Cheerios and Disney exist primarily to make money, not to provide them with fun.[16]

Encourage alternative activities to watching television and playing on the computer. Children's imagination and energy can be channeled into more healthy activities that will help them grow and satisfy their needs. In supporting such activities, we must recognize that they generally require more parental interaction and support than placing our kids in front of either a television or computer screen. Once again, we must rethink our own values as parents and how they contribute to the way we interact with our children. Do we really want to spend time building with blocks, kicking a soccer ball, or going on a hike? Or would we rather be shopping, working, or watching television alone? How do these preferences reflect our own values?

3. *Talk to your child about materialism.*   Talking with children in constructive ways about drugs, alcohol, and sex can reduce the likelihood that they will engage in these risky behaviors. Having thoughtful discussions about issues related to consumption, image, and money can also help children be less obsessed with these things. When children nag to buy something, discuss with them why they "need" it before you run out to make a purchase. Why is possession of the product so crucial? Does your child think it will help her be accepted by her peers? Is it because he wants you as a parent to demonstrate your love through a purchase? These are all excellent introductions to deeper discussions.

Talk to your children about money and how to use it responsibly. Help them learn about money's purpose by involving them in their own purchases. If something they want is expensive, let them pay for half of it. Earning money will help them see what is involved before consumption and may lead them to wonder whether those new sneakers are really worth all the extra chores. Helping children to establish savings accounts can also improve their understanding of how important it is to save money for the future. And encouraging them to give to charity establishes an important precedent for more generous ways of using money and possessions.

Teach your children that almost everything they see in the media has an ulterior motive, and that motive is almost always to make money. Help children to see the underlying messages in advertisements and how marketers are attempting to manipulate them. Make watching advertisements into a game to see who can spot the most tricks of the trade in an advertisement. Point out how ridiculous most of the messages are. Recognize also that young children do not understand that the cartoon they see on a television program is actually different from the cartoon they see in an advertisement. Help them to know the difference.

4. *Band together with other parents.*   Part of the difficulty of the materialistic world is that Johnny next door already has the hot new game and "all the kids" are wearing a particular style of clothing. This is the juvenile version of keeping up with the Joneses.

To the extent that like-minded groups of parents can work together, a new type of comparison group can be formed, and you will not be alone in the desert of purportedly uncaring parents who refuse to buy the latest computer game. Instead, your child will recognize that you are not the only "weird" parent who puts other values above material goods and pursuits.

5. *Change what is happening in our schools.*   As children enter school, their social world broadens and the messages they receive about the worth of consumption increase in intensity. As children spend more time with peers, the pressures become immense to own the right items and to have the right image. Discuss with teachers and school board members ways to decrease these pressures. For example, in the United States, some maintain that one reason for making children wear school uniforms is that less emphasis is placed on what they wear and more is on learning.

Investigate whether your school district is among those directly pushing materialistic messages in its curricula, activities, and environment. Over 8 million children in 12,000 U.S. schools watch Channel One, which purports to be ten minutes of news directly relevant to children.[17] What is less recognized is that it also contains two minutes of commercials. Not only is watching Channel One taking away time from the knowledge teachers might impart, it also sends the message that the school system believes watching television and advertisements is important.

Another way schools support materialistic values is by forming alliances with companies to pay for equipment. For example, some computer companies offer schools free computers and Internet browsers in return for the opportunity to track where children go on the Internet. Profiles of what children like to see are then developed and sold to advertisers and marketers.[18] Another example of how corporate influences have made their way into schools can be seen in the case of exclusive contracts with soft-drink manufacturers, where companies offer bonuses for high sales of soda in schools on the condition that other drinks (including healthy ones like juice) are not sold in the building.

Companies want to sell their products in schools because they know they have a "captive audience." The truth of this statement becomes even more evident in cases where students are punished for rebelling against corporate infringement into their environments. In one case in Ohio, two teenagers who walked out of their classroom to protest Channel One were sent by their principal to a detention center for the day.[19] In Georgia, on a day when a high school was trying to win award money from Coca-Cola by engaging in the highly educational task of lining up to spell out the word "Coke," one student was suspended for wearing a T-shirt with a Pepsi logo.[20] These examples suggest that privacy, good nutrition, and freedom of expression may all be damaged when schools are infiltrated by corporations.

Parents do not have to allow schools to push materialistic values. By joining parent-teacher-school associations and becoming involved in school board decisions, we can influence the messages that our children receive. Of course, some administrators will say that they would not have enough televisions, computers, or gym equipment if they did not form partnerships with corporations. If this is so, we must confront the question of why schools are underfunded while corporations have so much money to "donate."

Societal Change

The task of changing society can seem overwhelming, as materialism is so deeply ingrained in our culture, the powers invested in maintaining society's consumerism appear omnipotent, and the possibilities of change always involve risk. Add to these the entrepreneur's lament: "If people don't consume as much and work so hard, the economy will collapse." Recession and depression are the hells of the capitalist, consumer belief system, while purchase and an ever-expanding economy are the routes to heaven.

Perhaps better heavens await different value systems, however. As noted earlier, our ideal of Utopia depends on our values. From a material-istic standpoint, Utopia is a place where there are plenty of goods to consume in large shopping malls. But from the standpoint of intrinsic values, it is a place where people feel secure and competent, feel free to be who they are, and feel connected to others and the community. The possibility of reaching this healthier vision of society, as we have seen, is undermined by materialistic values.

To this end, I suggest the following.

1. *Regulate advertisements.*   A person can go almost nowhere in the United States without encountering advertisements. Ads are an essential part of contemporary media, including television, radio, and print publications. While browsing the Internet, ads pop up on computer screens. They precede movies and line highways. They are affixed to the walls of sports stadiums, buses and bus benches in cities, and placards above urinals. Ads are even inside fortune cookies and pasted to pieces of fruit. Escaping them is well-nigh impossible.

I believe we should work to declare advertising-free zones. At the top of my list would be schools, roadways, and public spaces such as subways and buses. Some states have already moved in this direction, deciding that scenery is more important than billboards telling us how far it is to the next McDonald's. Some countries and several cities recognize that art in a subway station is far more edifying than ads. Which option we choose is a clear value choice: materialism or aesthetics.

We also have to work to decrease the amount of television advertising directed at children. A couple of European nations have taken such steps. In Greece, advertising of toys to children is banned between 7:00 A.M. and 10:00 P.M. No advertising targeted at children under twelve is allowed in Sweden or Norway.[21] If such regulation might seem impossible to implement in the United States, consider that in the 1970s the Federal Trade Commission proposed a similar ban based on research showing that most young children do not understand the purposes of advertising. The United States Congress responded by overruling the ban and then punished the commission by limiting its powers.[22] The issue could be revisited and reconsidered; all it would take is members of Congress to consider the good of the nation's children over the good of the nation's corporations. Again, this represents a clear value choice.

2. *Pursue legal strategies against advertising and media industries.*   An even bolder step would be to consider advertisements as a form of pollu-

tion. Water, air, and noise pollution are considered problematic when people have no choice but to drink filthy water, breathe dirty air, or hear deafening sounds, to the detriment of their health. Advertisements appear to be detrimental to people's well-being. Just as the government taxes companies that spurt noxious chemicals from their smokestacks, perhaps we should assess a tax on advertisers who spew materialistic messages. Some might cry that this limits freedom of speech, but as my friend Allen Kanner pointed out, we must always wonder about the relevance of free speech when companies pay thousands of dollars per second to display their messages.

Taking the analogy further, companies are frequently sued when they pollute or sell dangerous products. In the United States tobacco companies are paying billions of dollars in damages for cancers and other diseases caused by smoking. These companies sold a harmful product and they knowingly manipulated nicotine levels to make the products especially addictive. If someone filed a lawsuit against major advertising and marketing firms, and a subpoena was successfully issued that forced these firms to turn over their research on marketing strategies, I believe we would find many parallels to cigarette companies. Specifically, we might discover that some companies are very aware that their advertisements increase people's frustrations and dissatisfaction. Furthermore, such records might show that viewers' feelings are intentionally manipulated to increase their motivation to purchase advertised products.

Imagine if such a lawsuit were successful and advertising and marketing companies found themselves in the same position as cigarette companies: they have to develop ads showing that their product is harmful. Television shows would be interspersed with reminders that buying products will not really satisfy your psychological needs or make others love you in an authentic way. Instead, advertising companies would emphasize that any product's utility is limited to helping you get back and forth to the office or to removing spots from your clothes, but really nothing more. In addition, people in the agencies would be forced to turn their creative energies to developing programs to increase community contribution and personal growth, just as Phillip Morris now pays for programs to keep teenagers from starting the nicotine habit.

3. *Support corporations that are more intrinsically oriented.* Having just suggested we regulate and sue many of the nation's most powerful corporations, some readers may think I believe all corporations are evil and inhumane. Other things I have said in this book also might suggest that because companies and the capitalist economic system are most concerned with making money, they are by definition highly materialistic and thus less intrinsically oriented. This need not be the case. Some companies have corporate structures that support equality among workers through job tasks, salary structures, and profit sharing. Other companies have made significant strides in allowing employees opportunities to spend more time with their families (especially at crucial life junctures) and to improve their education. Still others place environmental responsibility at the forefront of their corporate concerns or include charitable giving as an essential component of their balance sheet, even allowing employees paid leave to volunteer for community organizations.

What these examples show is what I have been trying to emphasize in this book: materialism is relative. Materialistic values become unhealthy when they are highly important in comparison with other values for which we might strive. The question is one of balance, and these examples show that corporations may be able to balance their materialistic aims with healthier, more intrinsically oriented ones. The key will be to help corporations recognize that their best interests lie in attaining this balance, and that making money for themselves and their stockholders need not be their sole, or even primary, mandate. Corporations could instead be seen as organizations designed to encourage the health of their employees, to contribute to the welfare of their community, and to help heal the earth. This would no doubt be a clear change in orientation for some companies, but not an impossible one.

Policies of corporations can be influenced by many different types of people, including those who consume their products, shareholders, and employees. As consumers, we can choose to patronize only companies whose values reflect nonmaterialistic concerns embodied in intrinsic values; as such, companies with strong materialistic values will feel pressure to change or go out of business. As investors, we can follow the trend of socially responsible investments and divest ourselves of stocks that are held in companies driven primarily by materialistic values. Through these means, we can send corporations the message that they must consider more than just the "bottom line," and that other values, including equality, diversity, and ecological health, are just as, if not more, important. Of course, researching company policies and basing our purchases and investments on what we find requires time and energy on our own part. Choosing to support socially responsible companies may occasionally mean spending more money on products and earning less from our investments. Again, we must ask ourselves if those are prices we are willing to pay.

We can also influence the corporate world as employees. For example, the next time you are offered a raise, you might consider asking instead for an extra week of vacation, a shorter work week, or better benefits to enhance your health and well-being. Not only will these nonmonetary rewards allow you more time to pursue other interests and be with your family and friends, but such requests will send the message to your employer that there are other, more important rewards than more money.

4. *Vote for governmental officials who realize that increasing national wealth will not increase our happiness.* As we have seen, once a nation's level of wealth rises to the point at which its citizens' basic needs for food, shelter, and security are met, further increases in wealth do little to improve their quality of life. As citizens, we must therefore recognize that a national agenda focused on economic growth will not improve the quality of our lives. Certainly we will have better and fancier products to consume, but our needs will not be better satisfied. For this reason, governments must be encouraged to implement policies that are less focused on economic growth and more concerned with other means of improving quality of life.

One step in the right direction would be to reconsider our national measures of "progress." Improvements in quality of life have been typically indexed by increases in a nation's gross national product or stock exchanges. Such financially based measures, however, are clearly inaccurate indicators of quality of life for more economically developed nations. Some forward-thinking economists and social scientists have developed alternative measures that are not based solely on materialistic issues, but take into consideration a broader array of statistical indicators to represent how well people are doing in life. For example, Redefining Progress and the Calvert-Henderson quality of life indicators include measures such as education, the environment, human rights, and recreation, among others, in an attempt to provide a more complex and accurate way of defining national progress.[23] If such indicators were considered together with the gross national product, government officials would have to recognize that the two do not go hand in hand. We could then begin to develop more programs to improve these truer indicators of progress at the same time that we place less focus on programs that primarily work from a definition of progress based in materialistic values.[24]

5. *Work to ensure everyone's security.* Chapter 4 suggested that poverty, by failing to satisfy people's needs for safety and sustenance, leads to both high materialism and low well-being. One solution for making the world less materialistic and improving happiness is therefore to eliminate poverty. Geoffrey Miller noted that for most people in the Western world "every hundred dollars that we spend on ourselves will have no detectable effect on our happiness; but the same money, if given to the hungry, ill, oppressed developing world people, would dramatically increase their happiness."[25] From the framework used in this book, the safety and sustenance needs of these individuals would be better satisfied, and thus their happiness raised. Of interest, such a strategy could also increase the well-being of people in the more economically developed world. By using money to create opportunities for those in more need, intrinsic values of contributing to the community would be expressed and reinforced, which should also improve the need satisfaction and well-being of those who give.

Solving the poverty problem is clearly not as simple as writing a check to every poor person, and improvements in the economy have obviously not led prosperity to trickle down equally to everyone. Certainly liberal and conservative policies alike must have the possibility of securing a better life for people in unfortunate social circumstances. To the extent we can share with each other, rather than concentrate wealth in the hands of a relative few, everyone's happiness might improve.

6. *Experiment with alternative economic systems.* With the fall of the Soviet Union and China's movement toward a free market, many have declared capitalism the clear winner of the competition of economic

systems. Yet there are costs to the capitalist system, including globalization, cultural (Western consumerism) homogeneity, decline of small businesses at the hands of chain stores, increasing gaps between rich and poor within and across nations, and the like. And that doesn't include problems associated with materialism described here.

Some communities are responding by experimenting with alternative economies based on currencies other than the almighty dollar.[26] Ithaca, New York, for example, has a very successful program of community money that can be exchanged only within a certain radius of the town. Other communities are establishing time banks in which people donate a number of hours of their services and then receive an equal number of hours of others' services in return; in such systems, the work of a lawyer is considered equal in value to that of a gardener. Another popular system is Local Exchange Trading System (LETS). Although the systems have certain differences, they all work on the basis of different values than the winner-take-all mentality of the global market. They work to support neighbors, are egalitarian in their sense of what people's time is worth, and are rarely used in ways that have the harmful social and environmental costs we saw in chapter 8. Although still economic systems, they reinforce many of what Shalom Schwartz called "universalism" values, or what my colleagues and I would term intrinsic pursuits.

Cooperatives are another fine example of alternative economic systems. In the United States we have been taught that individual ownership is ideal, as it purportedly provides the greatest independence and fewest barriers to expression of our individuality. From a marketing and business viewpoint, consumers must hold this attitude, for if five neighbors were to share the cost of a lawnmower, that would mean four fewer products had been sold. Libraries are one of the few widely accepted institutions in the United States that involve shared possessions. Yet the idea can be expanded to many different products that we only occasionally use. Some towns have tool cooperatives in which citizens can borrow a circular saw the two times a year they might need one. Other neighborhoods have community vegetable gardens where people share both weeding and harvesting. Purchasing products with neighbors is another way simultaneously to save money and build stronger community ties. Families can swap children's toys and books. Each of these practices can help us realize that products may be shared instead of individually owned, and thereby decrease materialism.

Summary

This final chapter suggests strategies for making changes in the personal, family, and societal processes that encourage materialistic values. I also tried to provide an alternative vision of values based on research showing that people are happier to the extent that they focus on values for self-acceptance, good relationships, and contributions to the community. To the extent we can break, both personally and collectively, some of the vicious cycles brought about by a focus on materialism, we will be able to improve the quality of life for ourselves, our families, our communities, and our planet.

Epilogue

I would like to end by retelling a story that I often read to my sons. It is a fable that conveys many of the ideas discussed in this book. The story was written by Marcus Pfister, and is called *The Rainbow Fish*.[1]

The Rainbow Fish was the most beautiful fish in the entire ocean, for he had shimmering, colorful scales. All the fish admired him, but the Rainbow Fish rarely played with them.

One day, a little blue fish asked the Rainbow Fish if he might have one of his shiny scales. The Rainbow Fish became annoyed and yelled at the little blue fish. Word of the incident spread through the sea, and soon no one would pay any attention to the Rainbow Fish.

With no one to admire him, the Rainbow Fish felt sad, so he sought the counsel of a wise octopus. The octopus advised the Rainbow Fish to share his scales with the other fish. She warned that he would no longer be the most beautiful fish in the ocean, but that he would be happy. Naturally, the Rainbow Fish doubted this advice.

But when the little blue fish returned and asked again for a scale, the Rainbow Fish hesitantly removed one of his smallest scales and gave it to the little fish. A new and peculiar feeling came over him. Soon, other fish appeared, and, one by one, the Rainbow Fish gave away his shiny scales, until he was surrounded by the shimmering from all the fish with whom he had shared.

Finally the Rainbow Fish had only one shining scale left. His most prized possessions had been given away, yet he was very happy.

"Come on Rainbow Fish," they called. "Come and play with us!"

"Here I come," said Rainbow Fish and, happy as a splash, he swam off to join his friends.

Notes

Chapter 1

1. Quotation from Lao Tzu (1988).

2. See Belk (1983) for more about religious and philosophical views on materialism.

3. Quotations from the wealthy are in Winokur (1996) and those from the poets are in Simpson (1988).

4. I first wrote about this contrast in Kasser (2000).

5. For more on these views, see Buss (1996).

6. See Bandura (1977) or Skinner (1972). Also, do not take these statements as suggesting that I reject all of the principles of evolutionary psychology or behaviorism. There is no doubt in my mind that natural selection and the principles of conditioning both play an important role in human behavior. My point is that some of the meta-theoretical assumptions of these viewpoints have been used in ways that support consumeristic and capitalistic messages.

7. See Buckley (1982) for more on Watson.

8. For more on the humanistic views, see Fromm (1976), Maslow (1954), and Rogers (1961).

9. Quotation is from Myers and Diener (1996), pp. 70–71.

Chapter 2

1. Carnegie quotation is from Hendrick (1932), pp. 146–147.

2. There is no real agreement in psychology as to the exact number or content of values that make up the human value system, although Shalom Schwartz (1992, 1994, 1996) has made an excellent case for a "universal" system of values. Nonetheless, a glance through a review of value measures (Braithwaite & Scott 1991) will probably impress the reader for how much disagreement exists among psychologists about what values are important to measure.

3. This first study is Kasser and Ryan (1993).

4. Milton Rokeach (1973), a prominent thinker in empirical value research, coined the term "relative centrality" to describe how important a value is relative to other values. His insistence on this means of measurement is relatively well accepted among value researchers.

5. Maslow (1954) described this idea well.

6. Well-being measures include self-actualization (Jones & Crandall, 1986), vitality (Ryan & Frederick, 1997), anxiety (Derogatis et al., 1974), and depression (Radloff, 1977).

7. The scales in this study were social productivity (Ikle et al., 1983), conduct disorders (Herjanic & Reich, 1982), and global functioning (American Psychiatric Association, 1987). See Sameroff et al. (1982) for more information about the heterogeneous sample.

8. Further information on results from the next two samples reviewed can be found in Kasser (1994) or Kasser and Ryan (1996).

9. See Ryan et al. (1999) and Schmuck et al. (2000).

10. Items were taken from Emmons (1991).

11. Another important finding from this study related to an issue relevant to socially desirable responding. Psychologists are often concerned that participants' responses to certain questionnaires are clouded by the desire to answer in a way that fits with what they think society feels is "good." As a result, they may be unlikely to admit to feelings and thoughts that might be seen as deviant or less than optimal. Because a scale exists to measure socially desirable responding (Crowne & Marlowe, 1960), we examined whether this might explain why people strongly focused on materialistic values reported low well-being. Our statistical analyses found no support for this idea, as the effects remained significant even after accounting for socially desirable responses. Notably, however, Mick (1996) reached a different conclusion with other measures of materialism.

12. See Cushman (1990) or Kanner and Gomes (1995).

13. This narcissism scale was developed by Raskin and Terry (1988).

14. Kasser and Ryan (2001).

15. Williams et al. (2000).

16. Goal measures are based on Emmons (1989) and Little (1983).

17. Sheldon and Kasser (1995, 1998).

18. Sheldon and Kasser (2001).

19. Carver and Baird (1998), Srivastava et al. (2001), McHoskey (1999), and Roberts and Robins (2000), respectively.

20. The following study summarizes some of the results from Cohen and Cohen (1996).

21. See American Psychiatric Association (1987).

22. Cohen and Cohen (1996), p. 139.

23. Belk (1984, 1985).

24. Studies replicating life satisfaction results include Ahuvia and Wong (1995), Dawson (1988), and Dawson and Bamossy (1991); results for depression were reported by Wachtel and Blatt (1990) and for social anxiety by Schroeder and Dugal (1995).

25. Richins and Dawson (1992).

26. Studies replicating include Ahuvia and Wong (1995) and Mick (1996).

27. Results are from countries as follows: Britain (Chan & Joseph, 2000); Denmark and India (Khanna & Kasser, 2001); German students (Schmuck et al., 2000); German adults (Schmuck, 2001); Romania (Frost, 1998); Russia (Ryan et al., 1999); Singapore (Kasser & Ahuvia, 2002); and South Korea (Kim et al., in press). Notably, results from Singapore occurred for the Aspiration Index, the Richins and Dawson scale, and the Belk scale.

28. See Saunders and Munro (2000), Sirgy et al. (1995), Keng et al. (2000), Swinyard et al. (2001), and Diener and Oishi (2000).

29. The one study that may seemingly conflict with this statement is by Sagiv and Schwartz (2000). These investigators found that business students highly focused on power values reported high well-being. They interpreted this as inconsistent with the body of work on materialistic values. As we (Kasser & Ahuvia, 2002) pointed out in response, power values are not the same as materialistic values; indeed, when we examined materialistic values using the Aspiration Index and the Belk and Richins and Dawson scales in samples of Singaporean business students, we confirmed our earlier findings that materialistic values are related to low well-being. Notably, Srivastava et al. (2001) reported parallel findings in United States business students and entrepreneurs.

Chapter 3

1. See, for example, McDougall (1908), Murray (1938), Maslow (1954), or Ryan and Deci (2000) for some of the most well-known conceptions. The list could go on.

2. See, for example, Bandura (1977).

3. The following definition owes much to the work of Ryan (1995).

4. Some readers will see the ideas of Maslow behind these needs, and I must certainly acknowledge that my thinking has been greatly influenced by him. Maslow's ideas involved a hierarchical arrangement in which certain needs did not obtain much force until lower-level needs had been reasonably well met. The research is clearly mixed on the validity of Maslow's hierarchy, and for this reason I present a theory of needs that does not make assumptions about their relative ordering or potency in motivating behavior.

5. Conceptions of security-safety needs can be seen from the evolutionary view in Buss (1996); from the psychodynamic in Becker (1973), Freud (1909/1961), Erikson (1959/1980), Horney (1950), and Pyszczynski et al. (1997); and from the humanistic in Maslow (1954) and Rogers (1961).

6. Conceptions of esteem-competence needs can be seen from the cybernetic-cognitive view in Bandura (1977), Carver and Scheier (1982), and Locke and Latham (1990); from the psychodynamic in Erikson (1959/1980), Murray (1938), and White (1959); from social psychologists in Aronson (1992), Epstein (1990), and Solomon et al. (1991); and from humanists in Deci and Ryan (1985, 1991), Maslow (1954), and Rogers (1961).

7. Conceptions of connectedness needs can be seen from the evolutionary view in Bowlby (1969/1982) and Buss (1996); from psychodynamic and object relations theorists in Bakan (1966), Erikson (1959/1980), and Greenberg and Mitchell (1983); from social psychology by Baumeister and Leary (1995), Epstein (1990), Hazan and Shaver (1987), McAdams and Bryant (1987), and Reis and Patrick (1996); and from humanists in Deci and Ryan (1985, 1991), Maslow (1954), and Rogers (1961).

8. Conceptions of needs for autonomy, freedom, and intrinsic motivation can be found in Bakan (1966), Csikszentmihalyi (1997, 1999), deCharms (1968), Deci and Ryan (1985, 1991), Laing (1960), Maslow (1954), May (1967), and Rogers (1961).

9. See Feather (1992, 1995) and Emmons (1989).

10. For parents, see Kasser et al. (1995); for television, see Cheung and Chan (1996), Kasser and Ryan (2001), and Moschis and Moore (1982).

11. More on this can be found in Kasser et al. (in press).

12. Quotation is from Maslow (1954), p. 82.

Chapter 4

1. Tolkien (1977), pp. 328–329.

2. See Maslow (1954), Fromm (1976), Rogers (1964), and Inglehart (1977).

3. Kasser et al. (1995).

4. The interview was based on Brown and Rutter (1966), and the survey was devised by Sameroff et al. (1989).

5. Williams et al. (2000), Cohen and Cohen (1996).

6. Rindfleisch et al. (1997).

7. Rindfleisch et al. (1997), p. 321.

8. Kasser et al. (1995).

9. Cohen and Cohen (1996).

10. Inglehart (1971) is a good place to start for the theory behind his ideas.

11. See Inglehart and Abramson (1994) and Abramson and Inglehart (1995) for data relevant to these three findings.

12. See Stewart and Healy (1989) for an interesting theoretical discussion of some similar issues.

13. Ann Slater's quotation is from Winokur (1996).

14. See Feingold (1992) for a meta-analysis supporting this conclusion.

15. Buss (1989) develops the evolutionary idea, and Caporael (1989) expresses the social view.

16. Kasser and Sharma (1999).

17. Data from Buss et al. (1990).

18. Kasser and Kasser (2001).

19. Van de Castle (1993).

20. See Becker's (1973) classic *The Denial of Death* and Solomon et al. (1991) for the basics of these ideas.

21. Kasser and Sheldon (2000).

Chapter 5

1. Quotation is from Kurt Anderson's article in the *New York Times Review of Books* (1999) about *The New New Thing,* by Michael Lewis. Clark's actual statements can be found in Lewis (2000), pp. 259–261.

2. Diener et al. (1993).

3. Brickman et al. (1978).

4. Figure 5.1 is from Myers (2000).

5. European data from Easterlin (1995) and Japanese data from Diener and Oishi (2000).

6. Kasser and Ryan (2001).

7. Ryan et al. (1999).

8. Sheldon and Kasser (1998).

9. See Baumeister (1993) for some perspectives.

10. Results are from Chan and Joseph (2000), Kasser and Ryan (2001), and Sheldon and Kasser (1995); self-esteem items are from Rosenberg (1965).

11. See, for example, Kernis and Paradise (2002) or Deci and Ryan (1995).

12. See Kanner and Gomes (1995), Kohut (1971), and Miller (1981).

13. Kasser and Kasser (2001).

14. See Carver et al. (1996) or Higgins (1987).

15. Khanna and Kasser (2001).

16. Results for Denmark and India from Khanna and Kasser (2001); for Hong Kong from Cheung and Chan (1996); for Finland from Murphy (2000); for Australia from Saunders and Munro (2000); and for the United States from Kasser and Ryan (2001).

17. See Richins (1992, 1995) or Sirgy (1998) for more on social comparison and materialism.

18. See Rahtz et al. (1988a, 1989)

19. Sirgy et al. (1998).

20. Richins (1991).

21. Braun and Wicklund (1989).

22. Getty quotation is from Winokur (1996).

23. Kapteyn and Wansbeek (1982).

24. See, for example, Hirschman (1992).

Chapter 6

1. Hammer quotation is from Winokur (1996).

2. See note 7 in chapter 3 for a start.

3. See Putnam (2000).

4. See Lane (2000), p. 9.

5. Kasser and Ryan (2001).

6. Sheldon and Flanagan (2001); conflict survey is from Straus (1979).

7. Khanna and Kasser (2001); the additional scale was developed by Moschis (1978).

8. McHoskey (1999).

9. See Kasser and Kasser (2001).

10. Kasser and Ryan (1993); Cohen and Cohen (1996), p. 49, table 3.3; Keng et al. (2000); Richins and Dawson (1992). Ryan et al. (1999) and Schmuck et al. (2000) present parallel results in Russia and Germany.

11. Schwartz and Sagiv (1995).

12. See Schwartz (1992, 1994, 1996) for more.

13. Goldberg and Gorn (1978).

14. Schwartz (1992), p. 15.

15. This notion of objectification stems largely from writers such as Buber (1958), Fromm (1955), Laing (1967), and B. Schwartz (1994).

16. Cerbin (2000).

17. Ahuvia and Adelman (1993)

18. Richins and Dawson (1992); McHoskey (1999).

19. Results from Sheldon and Kasser (1995); empathy survey is from Davis (1980).

20. B. Schwartz (1994), p. 201.

21. Khanna and Kasser (2001).

22. See Christie and Geis (1970).

23. McHoskey (1999).

24. Sheldon et al. (2000); more information on the Prisoner's Dilemma game can be found in Komorita and Parks (1994).

25. Quotation is from Sheldon et al. (2000), p. 400.

Chapter 7

1. Fromm (1941), pp. 109–110.

2. See Rogers (1961), Fromm (1941), Deci and Ryan (1985, 1991), Ryan (1995), Vallerand (1997), and Maddi et al. (1982).

3. Quote from Deci (1995), p. 2.

4. See Ryan et al. (1993) for more on feelings of autonomy and religious behavior.

5. See Abramson and Inglehart (1995), Cohen and Cohen (1996), and Kasser and Ryan (1996).

6. See Schwartz (1992, 1994, 1996) or Schwartz and Sagiv (1995).

7. See Csikszentmihalyi (1997), Deci and Ryan (1985, 1991), or Vallerand (1997).

8. Deci (1971).

9. See Deci and Ryan (1985, 1991) for general reviews and Deci et al. (1999) for the meta-analysis.

10. Khanna and Kasser (2001).

11. Amabile et al. (1994).

12. Sheldon et al. (2001).

13. See Gibbons (1990).

14. Plant and Ryan (1985); see also Lepper and Greene (1975).

15. See Schroeder and Dugal (1995); self-consciousness items come from Fenigstein et al. (1975).

16. Kubey and Csikszentmihalyi (1990); Delle Fave and Bassi (2000); Massimini et al. (1992).

17. Delle Fave, personal communication (2000).

18. Schor (1992, 1998).

19. This table and the basic definitions are taken primarily from Ryan (1995), and are based on earlier work of Ryan and Connell (1989), among others. Substantial evidence showing how these reasons relate to well-being can be found in those articles, as well as in Ryan et al. (1993), Sheldon and Kasser (1995, 1998), and Sheldon and Elliott (1999).

20. See Sheldon and Kasser (1995, 1998, 2001).

21. Richins (1994).

22. Srivastava et al. (2001).

23. See Christenson et al. (1994), Faber and O'Guinn (1988, 1992), McElroy et al. (1995), and O'Guinn and Faber (1989). Quotations that follow are primarily from O'Guinn and Faber (1989).

Chapter 8

1. Quotation is from Winokur (1996).

2. See Amato and Rogers (1997) or Koutstaal (1998) for work on finances and marital conflict.

3. Rohan and Zanna (1996).

4. Kasser et al. (1995).

5. Kasser et al. (1995).

6. See Winokur (1996), p. 23.

7. B. Schwartz (1994).

8. McNeal quotation from Seipp (2001); all others from Ruskin (1999).

9. Oskamp (2000).

10. Inglehart (1977).

11. Schwartz (1992, 1994, 1996).

12. Saunders and Munro (2000).

13. Richins and Dawson (1992).

14. Hardin (1968).

15. Sheldon and McGregor (2000).

Chapter 9

1. Quotation is from Al-Suhrawardy (1995), p. 110.

2. See Kasser (1994), Kasser and Ryan (1996), or Sheldon and Kasser (1995, 1998).

3. Kasser and Ryan (1993, 1996, 2001); Sheldon and Kasser (1995).

4. Kasser and Ryan (2001).

5. Kasser and Ryan (1993).

6. Sheldon and McGregor (2000).

7. Cohen and Cohen (1996), Diener and Oishi (2000).

8. Kasser and Ryan (1996), Sheldon and Kasser (2001).

9. Diener and Oishi (2000), Ryan et al. (1999), Schmuck et al. (2000).

10. Kasser and Ryan (2001), Sheldon and Kasser (1998).

11. Elgin (1993), Etzioni (1998).

12. Grube et al. (1994), Rokeach (1968, 1971).

13. Kottler (1999), Money, Meaning, and Choices Institute (n.d.).

14. Astin et al. (1987), Sax et al. (1998); Myers (2000) summarizes this data.

15. American Academy of Pediatrics (1999).

16. Center for a New American Dream (n.d.)

17. Ruskin (1999).

18. Ruskin (1999).

19. Strickland (2001).

20. *New York Times* (1998).

21. Ruskin (1999).

22. Ruskin (1999).

23. Henderson et al. (2000), Redefining Progress (n.d.).

24. See Diener (2000) for more.

25. Miller (2000).

26. Web-based *International Journal of Community Currency Research* summarizes a variety of different types of studies and information on these topics.

Epilogue

1. The story is from Pfister (1992). The final quotation is on the last page, which is unnumbered.

References

Abramson, P. R., & Inglehart, R. (1995). *Value change in global perspective.* Ann Arbor: University of Michigan Press.

Ahuvia, A. C., & Adelman, M. B. (1993). Market metaphors for meeting mates. *Research in Consumer Behavior, 6,* 55–83.

Ahuvia, A. C., & Wong, N. (1995). Materialism: Origins and implications for personal well-being. In F. Hansen (Ed.), *European advances in consumer research,* Vol. 2 (pp. 172–178). Copenhagen, Denmark: Association for Consumer Research.

Al-Suhrawardy, A. (1995). *The sayings of Muhammad.* New York: Carol Publishing Group.

Amabile, T. M., Hill, K. G., Hennessey, B. A., & Tight, E. M. (1994). The work preference inventory: Assessing intrinsic and extrinsic motivational orientations. *Journal of Personality and Social Psychology, 66,* 950–967.

Amato, P. R., & Rogers, S. J. (1997). A longitudinal study of marital problems and subsequent divorce. *Journal of Marriage and the Family, 59,* 612–624.

American Academy of Pediatrics. (1999). Policy statement on media education. *Pediatrics, 104,* 341–343.

American Psychiatric Association. (1987). *Diagnostic and statistical manual of mental disorders* (3rd ed., rev.). Washington, DC: American Psychiatric Association.

Anderson, K. (1999). Valley guy. *New York Times Review of Books,* October 31.

Aronson, E. (1992). *The social animal.* New York: Freeman.

Astin, A. W., Green, K. C., & Korn, W. S. (1987). *The American freshman: Twenty year trends.* Los Angeles: Higher Education Research Institute, Graduate School of Education, University of California, Los Angeles.

Bakan, D. (1966). *The duality of human existence: Isolation and communion in Western man.* Boston: Beacon.

Bandura, A. (1977). Self-efficacy: Toward a unifying theory of behavioral change. *Psychological Review, 84,* 191–215.

Baumeister, R. (Ed.). (1993). *Self-esteem: The puzzle of low self-regard.* New York: Plenum Press.

Baumeister, R., & Leary, M. R. (1995). The need to belong: Desire for interpersonal attachments as a fundamental human motivation. *Psychological Bulletin, 117,* 497–529.

Becker, E. (1973). *The denial of death.* New York: Free Press.

Belk, R. W. (1983). Worldly possessions: Issues and criticisms. In R. P. Bagozzi & A. M. Tybout (Eds.), *Advances in consumer research,* Vol. 10 (pp. 514–519). Ann Arbor, MI: Association for Consumer Research.

Belk, R. W. (1984). Three scales to measure constructs related to materialism: Reliability, validity, and relationships to measures of happiness. In T. Kinnear (Ed.), *Advances in consumer research,* Vol. 11 (pp. 291–297). Provo, UT: Association for Consumer Research.

Belk, R. W. (1985). Materialism: Trait aspects of living in the material world. *Journal of Consumer Research, 12,* 265–280.

Bowlby, J. (1969/1982). *Attachment* (2nd ed.). New York: Basic Books.

Braithwaite, V. A., & Scott, W. A. (1991). Values. In J. P. Robinson, P. R. Shaver, & L. S. Wrightsman (Eds.), *Measures of personality and social psychological attitudes* (pp. 661–753). San Diego: Academic Press.

Braun, O. L., & Wicklund, R. A. (1989). Psychological antecedents of conspicuous consumption. *Journal of Economic Psychology, 10,* 161–187.

Brickman, P., Coates, D., & Janoff-Bulman, R. (1978). Lottery winners and accident victims: Is happiness relative? *Journal of Personality and Social Psychology, 36,* 917–927.

Brown, G. N., & Rutter, M. (1966). The measurement of family activities and relationships: A methodological study. *Human Relations, 19,* 214–263.

Buber, M. (1958). *I and thou* (2nd ed.). New York: Scribner.

Buckley, K. W. (1982). The selling of a psychologist: John Broadus Watson and the application of behavioral techniques to advertising. *Journal of the History of the Behavioral Sciences, 18,* 207–221.

Buss, D. M. (1989). Sex differences in human mate preferences: Evolutionary hypotheses tested in 37 cultures. *Behavioral and Brain Sciences, 12,* 1–49.

Buss, D. M. (1996). The evolutionary psychology of human social strategies. In E. T. Higgins & A. W. Kruglanski (Eds.), *Social psychology: Handbook of basic principles* (pp. 3–38). New York: Guilford Press.

Buss, D. M., et al. (1990). International preferences in selecting mates: A study of 37 cultures. *Journal of Cross-Cultural Psychology, 21,* 5–47.

Caporael, L. R. (1989). Mechanisms matter: The difference between sociobiology and evolutionary psychology [commentary on Buss, 1989]. *Behavioral and Brain Sciences, 12,* 17–18.

Carver, C. S., & Baird, E. (1998). The American dream revisited: Is it what you want or why you want it that matters? *Psychological Science, 9,* 289–292.

Carver, C. S., Lawrence, J. W., & Scheier, M. F. (1996). A control-process perspective on the origins of affect. In L. L. Martin & A. Tesser (Eds.), *Striving and feeling: Interactions among goals, affect, and self-regulation* (pp. 11–52). Mahwah, NJ: Erlbaum.

Carver, C. S., & Scheier, M. F. (1982). Control theory: A useful conceptual framework for personality, social, clinical, and health psychology. *Psychological Bulletin, 92,* 111–135.

Center for a New American Dream (n.d.). *Tips for parenting in a consumer culture.* Takoma Park, MD: Author.

Cerbin, C. (2000). Move over, Mary Poppins. *American Way,* October issue, p. 54.

Chan, R., & Joseph, C. (2000). Dimensions of personality, domains of aspiration, and subjective well-being. *Personality and Individual Differences, 28,* 347–354.

Cheung, C., & Chan, C. (1996). Television viewing and mean world value in Hong Kong's adolescents. *Social Behavior and Personality, 24,* 351–364.

Christenson, G. A., Faber, R. J., deZwann, M., Raymond, N. C., Specker, S. M., Ekern, M. D., Mackenzie, T. B., Crosby, R. D., Crow, S. J., Eckert, E. D., Mussell, M. P., & Mitchell, J. E. (1994). Compulsive buying: Descriptive characteristics and psychiatric comorbidity. *Journal of Clinical Psychiatry, 55,* 5–11.

Christie, R., & Geis, F. L. (1970). *Studies in Machiavellianism.* New York: Academic Press.

Cohen, P., & Cohen, J. (1996). *Life values and adolescent mental health.* Mahwah, NJ: Erlbaum.

Crowne, D. P., & Marlowe, D. (1960). A new scale of social desirability independent of psychopathology. *Journal of Consulting Psychology, 24,* 349–354.

Csikszentmihalyi, M. (1997). *Finding flow.* New York: Basic Books.

Csikszentmihalyi, M. (1999). If we are so rich, why aren't we happy? *American Psychologist, 54,* 821–827.

Cushman, P. (1990). Why the self is empty: Toward a historically situated psychology. *American Psychologist, 45,* 599–611.

Davis, M. H. (1980). A multidimensional approach to individual differences in empathy. *JSAS Catalog of Selected Documents in Psychology, 10,* 85 (Ms. no. 2124).

Dawson, S. (1988). Trait materialism: Improved measures and an extension to multiple domains of life satisfaction. In S. Shapiro & A. H. Walle (Eds.), *AMA Winter Educators Conference Proceedings* (pp. 478–481). Chicago: American Marketing Association.

Dawson, S., & Bamossy, G. (1991). If we are what we have, what are we when we don't have? *Journal of Social Behavior and Personality, 6*, 363–384.

deCharms, R. (1968). *Personal causation: The internal affective determinants of behavior.* New York: Academic Press.

Deci, E. L. (1971). Effects of externally mediated rewards on intrinsic motivation. *Journal of Personality and Social Psychology, 18*, 105–115.

Deci, E. L. (1995). *Why we do what we do.* New York: G. P. Putnam's Sons.

Deci, E. L., Koestner, R., & Ryan, R. M. (1999). A meta-analytic review of experiments examining the effects of extrinsic rewards on intrinsic motivation. *Psychological Bulletin, 125*, 627–668.

Deci, E. L., & Ryan, R. M. (1985). *Intrinsic motivation and self-determination in human behavior.* New York: Plenum Press.

Deci, E. L., & Ryan, R. M. (1991). A motivational approach to self: Integration in personality. In R. Dienstbier (Ed.), *Nebraska symposium on motivation, Vol. 38. Perspectives on motivation* (pp. 237–288). Lincoln: University of Nebraska Press.

Deci, E. L., & Ryan, R. M. (1995). Human autonomy: The basis for true self-esteem. In M. Kernis (Ed.), *Efficacy, agency, and self-esteem* (pp. 31–49). New York: Plenum Press.

Delle Fave, A., & Bassi, M. (2000). The quality of experience in adolescents' daily life: Developmental perspectives. *Genetic, Social, and General Psychology Monographs, 126*, 347–367.

Derogatis, L. R., Lipman, R. S., Rickels, K., Uhlenhuth, E. H., & Covi, L. (1974). The Hopkins Symptom Checklist (HSCL): A self-report symptom inventory. *Behavioral Science, 19*, 1–15.

Diener, E. (2000). Subjective well-being: The science of happiness and a proposal for a national index. *American Psychologist, 55*, 34–43.

Diener, E., & Oishi, S. (2000). Money and happiness: Income and subjective well-being across nations. In E. Diener & E. M. Suh (Eds.), *Subjective well-being across cultures* (pp. 185–218). Cambridge: MIT Press.

Diener, E., Sandvik, E., Seidlitz, L., & Diener, M. (1993). The relationship between income and subjective well-being: Relative or absolute? *Social Indicators Research, 28*, 195–223.

Easterlin, R. (1995). Will raising the incomes of all increase the happiness of all? *Journal of Economic Behavior and Organization, 27*, 35–47.

Elgin, D. (1993). *Voluntary simplicity.* New York: Morrow.

Emmons, R. A. (1989). The personal strivings approach to personality. In L. A. Pervin (Ed.), *Goal concepts in personality and social psychology* (pp. 87–126). Hillsdale, NJ: Erlbaum.

Emmons, R. A. (1991). Personal strivings, daily life events, and psychological and physical well-being. *Journal of Personality, 59*, 453–472.

Epstein, S. (1990). Cognitive-experiential self-theory. In L. A. Pervin (Ed.), *Handbook in personality: Theory and research* (pp. 165–191). New York: Guilford Press.

Erikson, E. (1959/1980). *Identity and the life cycle.* New York: Norton.

Etzioni, A. (1998). Voluntary simplicity: Characterization, select psychological implications, and societal consequences. *Journal of Economic Psychology, 19,* 619–643.

Faber, R. J., & O'Guinn, T. C. (1988). Compulsive consumption and credit abuse. *Journal of Consumer Policy, 11,* 97–109.

Faber, R. J., & O'Guinn, T. C. (1992). A clinical screener for compulsive buying. *Journal of Consumer Research, 19,* 459–469.

Feather, N. T. (1992). Values, valences, expectations, and actions. *Journal of Social Issues, 48,* 109–124.

Feather, N. T. (1995). Values, valences, and choice: The influence of values on the perceived attractiveness and choice of alternatives. *Journal of Personality and Social Psychology, 68,* 1135–1151.

Feingold, A. (1992). Gender differences in mate selection preferences: A test of the parental investment model. *Psychological Bulletin, 112,* 125–139.

Fenigstein, A., Scheier, M. F., & Buss, A. H. (1975). Public and private self-consciousness: Assessment and theory. *Journal of Consulting and Clinical Psychology, 43,* 522–527.

Freud, S. (1909/1961). *Five lectures on psycho-analysis.* New York: Norton.

Fromm, E. (1941). *Escape from freedom.* New York: Rinehart.

Fromm, E. (1955). *The sane society.* New York: Fawcett.

Fromm, E. (1976). *To have or to be?* New York: Harper & Row.

Frost, K. M. (1998). *A cross-cultural study of major life aspirations and psychological well-being.* Unpublished doctoral dissertation, University of Texas at Austin.

Gibbons, F. X. (1990). Self-attention and behavior: A review and theoretical update. In M. P. Zanna (Ed.), *Advances in experimental social psychology,* Vol. 23 (pp. 249–303). San Diego: Academic Press.

Goldberg, M. E., & Gorn, G. J. (1978). Some unintended consequences of TV advertising to children. *Journal of Consumer Research, 5,* 22–29.

Greenberg, J. R., & Mitchell, S. A. (1983). *Object relations in psychoanalytic theory.* Cambridge: Harvard University Press.

Grube, J. W., Mayton, D. M., & Ball-Rokeach, S. J. (1994). Inducing change in values, attitudes, and behaviors: Belief system theory and the method of value self-confrontation. *Journal of Social Issues, 50,* 153–173.

Hardin, G. (1968). The tragedy of the commons. *Science, 162,* 1243–1248.

Hazan, C., & Shaver, P. (1987). Romantic love conceptualized as an attachment process. *Journal of Personality and Social Psychology, 52,* 511–524.

Henderson, H., Lickerman, J., & Flynn, P. (Eds.). (2000). *Calvert-Henderson quality of life indicators.* Bethesda, MD: Calvert Group.

Hendrick, B. J. (1932). *The life of Andrew Carnegie,* Vol. 1. Garden City, NY: Doubleday.

Herjanic, B., & Reich, W. (1982). Development of a structured psychiatric interview for children: Agreement between child and parent on individual symptoms. *Journal of Abnormal Child Psychology, 10,* 307–324.

Higgins, E. T. (1987). Self-discrepancy: A theory relating self and affect. *Psychological Review, 94,* 319–340.

Hirschman, E. C. (1992). The consciousness of addiction: Toward a general theory of compulsive consumption. *Journal of Consumer Research, 19,* 155–179.

Horney, K. (1950). *Neurosis and human growth: The struggle toward self-realization.* New York: Norton.

Ikle, D. N., Lipp, D. O., Butters, E. A., & Ciarlo, J. (1983). *Development and validation of the adolescent community mental health questionnaire.* Denver, CO: Mental Systems Evaluation Project.

Inglehart, R. (1971). The silent revolution in Europe: Intergenerational change in post-industrial societies. *American Political Science Review, 65,* 991–1017.

Inglehart, R. (1977). *The silent revolution: Changing values and political styles among Western publics.* Princeton, NJ: Princeton University Press.

Inglehart, R., & Abramson, P. R. (1994). Economic security and value change. *American Political Science Review, 88,* 336–354.

International Journal of Community Currency Research (n.d.). http://www.geog.le.ac.uk/ijccr/index.html.

Jones, A., & Crandall, R. (1986). Validation of a short index of self-actualization. *Personality and Social Psychology Bulletin, 12,* 63–73.

Kanner, A. D., & Gomes, M. E. (1995). The all-consuming self. In T. Roszak, M. E. Gomes, & A. D. Kanner (Eds.), *Ecopsychology: Restoring the Earth, healing the mind* (pp. 77–91). San Francisco: Sierra Club Books.

Kapteyn, A., & Wansbeek, T. J. (1982). Empirical evidence on preference formation. *Journal of Economic Psychology, 2,* 137–154.

Kasser, T. (1994). *Further dismantling the American dream: Differential well-being correlates of intrinsic and extrinsic goals.* Unpublished doctoral dissertation, University of Rochester, Rochester, NY.

Kasser, T. (2002). Sketches for a self-determination theory of values. In E. L. Deci & R. M. Ryan (Eds.), *Handbook of self-determination research* (pp. 123–140). Rochester, NY: University of Rochester Press.

Kasser, T. (2000). Two versions of the American dream: Which goals and values make for a high quality of life? In E. Diener & D. R. Rahtz (Eds.), *Advances in quality of life theory and research,* Vol. 1 (pp. 3–12). Dordrecht, The Netherlands: Kluwer.

Kasser, T., & Ahuvia, A. C. (2002). Materialistic values and well-being in business students. *European Journal of Social Psychology, 32,* 137–146.

Kasser, T., & Kasser, V. G. (2001). The dreams of people high and low in materialism. *Journal of Economic Psychology, 22,* 693–719.

Kasser, T., Koestner, R., & Lekes, N. (in press). Early family experiences and adult values: A 26-year, prospective longitudinal study. *Personality and Social Psychology Bulletin.*

Kasser, T., & Ryan, R. M. (1993). A dark side of the American dream: Correlates of financial success as a central life aspiration. *Journal of Personality and Social Psychology, 65,* 410–422.

Kasser, T., & Ryan, R. M. (1996). Further examining the American dream: Differential correlates of intrinsic and extrinsic goals. *Personality and Social Psychology Bulletin, 22,* 280–287.

Kasser, T., & Ryan, R. M. (2001). Be careful what you wish for: Optimal functioning and the relative attainment of intrinsic and extrinsic goals. In P. Schmuck & K. M. Sheldon (Eds.), *Life goals and well-being: Towards a positive psychology of human striving* (pp. 116–131). Goettingen, Germany: Hogrefe & Huber.

Kasser, T., Ryan, R. M., Zax, M., & Sameroff, A. J. (1995). The relations of maternal and social environments to late adolescents' materialistic and prosocial values. *Developmental Psychology, 31,* 907–914.

Kasser, T., & Sharma, Y. (1999). Reproductive freedom, educational equality, and females' preference for resource acquisition characteristics in mates. *Psychological Science, 10,* 374–377.

Kasser, T., & Sheldon, K. M. (2000). Of wealth and death: Materialism, mortality salience, and consumption behavior. *Psychological Science, 11,* 352–355.

Keng, K. A., Jung, K., Jivan, T. S., & Wirtz, J. (2000). The influence of materialistic inclination on values, life satisfaction and aspirations: An empirical analysis. *Social Indicators Research, 49,* 317–333.

Kernis, M. H., & Paradise, A. W. (2002). Distinguishing between secure and fragile forms of high self-esteem. In E. L. Deci & R. M. Ryan (Eds.), *Handbook of self-determination research* (pp. 339–360). Rochester, NY: University of Rochester Press.

Khanna, S., & Kasser, T. (2001). *Materialism, objectification, and alienation from a cross-cultural perspective.*

Kim, Y., Kasser, T., & Lee, H. (in press). Self-concept, aspirations, and well-being in South Korea and the United States. *Journal of Social Psychology.*

Kohut, H. (1971). *The analysis of the self.* New York: International Universities Press.

Komorita, S., & Parks, C. (1994). *Social dilemmas*. Madison, WI: Brown & Benchmark, 1994.

Kottler, J. (1999). *Exploring and treating acquisitive desire*. Thousand Oaks, CA: Sage.

Koutstaal, S. W. (1998). *What's money got to do with it?: How financial issues relate to marital satisfaction*. Unpublished doctoral dissertation, Texas Tech University.

Kubey, R., & Csikszentmihalyi, M. (1990). *Television and the quality of life*. Hillsdale, NJ: Erlbaum.

Laing, R. D. (1960). *The divided self*. New York: Pantheon Books.

Laing, R. D. (1967). *The politics of experience*. New York: Ballantine Books.

Lane, R. E. (2000). *The loss of happiness in market democracies*. New Haven, CT: Yale University Press.

Lao Tzu (1988). *Tao Te Ching* (S. Mitchell, Trans.). New York: Harper & Row.

Lepper, M. R., & Greene, D. (1975). Turning play into work: Effects of adult surveillance and extrinsic rewards on children's intrinsic motivation. *Journal of Personality and Social Psychology, 31,* 479–486.

Lewis, M. (2000). *The new new thing: A Silicon Valley story*. New York: Norton.

Little, B. R. (1983). Personal projects: A rationale and method for investigation. *Environment and Behavior, 15,* 273–309.

Locke, E. A., & Latham, G. P. (1990). *A theory of goal setting and task performance*. Englewood Cliffs, NJ: Prentice Hall.

Maddi, S. R., Hoover, M., & Kobasa, S. C. (1982). Alienation and exploratory behavior. *Journal of Personality and Social Psychology, 42,* 884–890.

Maslow, A. H. (1954). *Motivation and personality*. New York: Harper & Row.

Massimini, F., Delle Fave, A., & Gaspardin, M. B. (1992). Televisione e qualita dell "esperienza soggettiva": l'integrazione tra dati quantitativi e qualitativi. *Ikon, 24,* 5–30.

May, R. (1967). *Psychology and the human dilemma*. New York: Norton.

McAdams, D. P., & Bryant, F. B. (1987). Intimacy motivation and subjective mental health in a nationwide sample. *Journal of Personality, 55,* 395–413.

McDougall, W. (1908). *Introduction to social psychology*. London: Methuen.

McElroy, S. L., Keck, P. E., & Phillips, K. A. (1995). Kleptomania, compulsive buying, and binge-eating disorder. *Journal of Clinical Psychiatry, 56,* 14–26.

McHoskey, J. W. (1999). Machiavellianism, intrinsic versus extrinsic goals, and social interest: A self-determination theory analysis. *Motivation and Emotion, 23,* 267–283.

Mick, D. G. (1996). Are studies of dark side variables confounded by socially desirable responding? The case of materialism. *Journal of Consumer Research, 23,* 106–119.

Miller, A. (1981). *The drama of the gifted child.* New York: Basic Books.

Miller, G. (2000). Social policy implications of the new happiness research. http://www.edge.org. February 16, 2000.

Money, Meaning, and Choices Institute (n.d.). http://www.mmcinstitute.com/index.html.

Moschis, G. P. (1978). *Acquisition of the consumer role by adolescents.* Atlanta: Georgia State University Publishing Services.

Moschis, G. P., & Moore, R. L. (1982). A longitudinal study of television advertising effects. *Journal of Consumer Research, 9,* 279–286.

Murphy, P. L. (2000). The commodified self in consumer culture: A cross-cultural perspective. *Journal of Social Psychology, 140,* 636–647.

Murray, H. (1938). *Explorations in personality.* New York: Oxford University Press.

Myers, D. G. (2000). The funds, friends, and faith of happy people. *American Psychologist, 55,* 56–67.

Myers, D. G., & Diener, E. (1996). The pursuit of happiness. *Scientific American, May,* 70–72.

New York Times. (March 26, 1998). A Pepsi fan is punished in Coke's backyard. p. D5.

O'Guinn, T. C., & Faber, R. J. (1989). Compulsive buying: A phenomenological exploration. *Journal of Consumer Research, 16,* 147–157.

Oskamp, S. (2000). A sustainable future for humanity? How can psychology help? *American Psychologist, 55,* 496–508.

Pfister, M. (1992). *The rainbow fish* (J. A. James, Trans.). New York: North-South Books.

Plant, R., & Ryan, R. M. (1985). Intrinsic motivation and the effects of self-consciousness, self-awareness and ego-involvement: An investigation of internally controlling styles. *Journal of Personality, 53,* 435–449.

Putnam, R. D. (2000). *Bowling alone: The collapse and revival of American community.* New York: Simon & Schuster.

Pyszczynski, T., Greenberg, J., & Solomon, S. (1997). Why do we need what we need? A terror management perspective on the roots of human social motivation. *Psychological Inquiry, 8,* 1–20.

Radloff, L. (1977). The CES-D scale: A self-report depression scale for research in the general population. *Applied Psychological Measurement, 1,* 385–401.

Rahtz, D. R., Sirgy, M. J., & Meadow, H. L. (1988a). Elderly life satisfaction and television viewership: An exploratory study. In M. J. Houston (Ed.), *Advances in consumer research,* Vol. 15 (pp. 141–145). Provo, UT: Association for Consumer Research.

Rahtz, D. R., Sirgy, M. J., & Meadow, H. L. (1988b). Elderly life satisfaction and television viewership: Replication and extension. In S. Shapiro & H. H. Walle

(Eds.), *1988 AMA winter educators' conference—Marketing: A return to the broader dimensions* (pp. 409–413). Chicago: American Marketing Association.

Rahtz, D. R., Sirgy, M. J., & Meadow, H. L. (1989). The elderly audience: Correlates of television orientation. *Journal of Advertising, 18,* 9–20.

Raskin, R., & Terry, H. (1988). A principal components analysis of the Narcissistic Personality Inventory and further evidence of its construct validity. *Journal of Personality and Social Psychology, 54,* 890–902.

Redefining Progress (n.d.). http://www.rprogress.org/.

Reis, H. T., & Patrick, B. C. (1996). Attachment and intimacy: Component processes. In E. T. Higgins & A. Kruglanski (Eds.), *Social psychology: Handbook of basic principles* (pp. 523–563). New York: Guilford Press.

Richins, M. L. (1991). Social comparison and the idealized images of advertising. *Journal of Consumer Research, 18,* 71–83.

Richins, M. L. (1992). Media images, materialism, and what ought to be: The role of social comparison. In F. Rudmin & M. L. Richins (Eds.), *Materialism: Meaning, measure, and morality* (pp. 202–206). Provo, UT: Association for Consumer Research.

Richins, M. L. (1994). Special possessions and the expression of material values. *Journal of Consumer Research, 21,* 522–533.

Richins, M. L. (1995). Social comparison, advertising, and consumer discontent. *American Behavioral Scientist, 38,* 593–607.

Richins, M. L., & Dawson, S. (1992). A consumer values orientation for materialism and its measurement: Scale development and validation. *Journal of Consumer Research, 19,* 303–316.

Rindfleisch, A., Burroughs, J. E., & Denton, F. (1997). Family structure, materialism, and compulsive consumption. *Journal of Consumer Research, 23,* 312–325.

Roberts, B. W., & Robins, R. W. (2000). Broad dispositions, broad aspirations: The intersection of personality traits and major life goals. *Personality and Social Psychology Bulletin, 26,* 1284–1296.

Rogers, C. R. (1961). *On becoming a person.* Boston: Houghton Mifflin.

Rogers, C. R. (1964). Toward a modern approach to values: The valuing process in the mature person. *Journal of Abnormal and Social Psychology, 68,* 160–167.

Rohan, M. J., & Zanna, M. P. (1996). Value transmission in families. In C. Seligman, J. M. Olson, & M. P. Zanna (Eds.), *Values: The Ontario symposium,* Vol. 8 (pp. 253–276). Hillsdale, NJ: Erlbaum.

Rokeach, M. (1968). *Beliefs, attitudes, and values.* San Francisco: Jossey-Bass.

Rokeach, M. (1971). Long range experimental modification of values, attitudes, and behavior. *American Psychologist, 26,* 453–459.

Rokeach, M. (1973). *The nature of human values.* New York: Free Press.

Rosenberg, M. (1965). *Society and the adolescent self-image.* Princeton, NJ: Princeton University Press.

Ruskin, G. (1999). Why they whine: How corporations prey on our children. *Mothering, (Nov-Dec)*, 41–50.

Ryan, R. M. (1995). Psychological needs and the facilitation of integrative processes. *Journal of Personality, 63*, 397–427.

Ryan, R. M., Chirkov, V. I., Little, T. D., Sheldon, K. M., Timoshina, E., & Deci, E. L. (1999). The American dream in Russia: Extrinsic aspirations and well-being in two cultures. *Personality and Social Psychology Bulletin, 25*, 1509–1524.

Ryan, R. M., & Connell, J. P. (1989). Perceived locus of causality and internalization: Examining reasons for acting in two domains. *Journal of Personality and Social Psychology, 57*, 749–761.

Ryan, R. M., & Deci, E. L. (2000). Self-determination theory and the facilitation of intrinsic motivation, social development, and well-being. *American Psychologist, 55*, 68–78.

Ryan, R. M., & Frederick, C. (1997). On energy, personality, and health: Subjective vitality as a dynamic reflection of well-being. *Journal of Personality, 65*, 529–565.

Ryan, R. M., Rigby, C. S., & King, K. (1993). Two types of religious internalization and their relations to religious orientation and mental health. *Journal of Personality and Social Psychology, 65*, 586–596.

Sagiv, L., & Schwartz, S. H. (2000). Value priorities and subjective well-being: Direct relations and congruity effects. *European Journal of Social Psychology, 30*, 177–198.

Sameroff, A. J., Seifer, R., & Zax, M. (1982). Early development of children at risk for emotional disorders. *Monographs of the Society for Research in Child Development, 47* (serial no. 199).

Sameroff, A. J., Thomas, S. L., & Barret, L. (1989). *Parental style survey*. Providence, RI: Bradley Hospital.

Saunders, S., & Munro, D. (2000). The construction and validation of a consumer orientation questionnaire (SCOI) designed to measure Fromm's (1955) "marketing character" in Australia. *Social Behavior and Personality, 28*, 219–240.

Sax, L. J., Astin, A. W., Korn, W. S., & Mahoney, K. M. (1998). *The American freshman: National norms for Fall, 1998*. Los Angeles: Higher Education Research Institute, University of California, Los Angeles.

Schmuck, P. (2001). Intrinsic and extrinsic life goals preferences as measured via inventories and via priming methodologies: Mean differences and relations with well-being. In P. Schmuck & K. M. Sheldon (Eds.), *Life goals and well-being: Towards a positive psychology of human striving* (pp. 132–147). Goettingen, Germany: Hogrefe & Huber.

Schmuck, P., Kasser, T., & Ryan, R. M. (2000). Intrinsic and extrinsic goals: Their structure and relationship to well-being in German and U.S. college students. *Social Indicators Research, 50*, 225–241.

Schor, J. (1992). *The overworked American: The unexpected decline of leisure.* New York: Basic Books.

Schor, J. (1998). *The overspent American: Upscaling, downshifting, and the new consumer.* New York: Basic Books.

Schroeder, J. E., & Dugal, S. S. (1995). Psychological correlates of the materialism construct. *Journal of Social Behavior and Personality, 10,* 243–253.

Schwartz, B. (1994). *The costs of living: How market freedom erodes the best things in life.* New York: Norton.

Schwartz, S. H. (1992). Universals in the content and structure of values: Theoretical and empirical tests in 20 countries. In M. Zanna (Ed.), *Advances in experimental and social psychology,* Vol. 25 (pp. 1–65). Orlando, FL: Academic Press.

Schwartz, S. H. (1994). Are there universal aspects in the content and structure of values? *Journal of Social Issues, 50,* 19–45.

Schwartz, S. H. (1996). Values priorities and behavior: Applying of theory of integrated value systems. In C. Seligman, J. M. Olson, & M. P. Zanna (Eds.), *The psychology of values: The Ontario symposium,* Vol. 8 (pp. 1–24). Hillsdale, NJ: Erlbaum.

Schwartz, S. H., & Sagiv, L. (1995). Identifying culture-specifics in the content and structure of values. *Journal of Cross-Cultural Psychology, 26,* 92–116.

Seipp, C. (2001). Kids: The new captive market. *Child* (September), 91–92, 150–152.

Sheldon, K. M., & Elliott, A. J. (1999). Goal-striving, need satisfaction, and well-being: The self-concordance model. *Journal of Personality and Social Psychology, 76,* 482–497.

Sheldon, K. M., Elliot, A. J., Kim, Y., & Kasser, T. (2001). What is satisfying about satisfying events?: Testing 10 candidate psychological needs. *Journal of Personality and Social Psychology, 80,* 325–339.

Sheldon, K. M., & Flanagan, M. (2001). *Extrinsic value orientation and dating violence.*

Sheldon, K. M., & Kasser, T. (1995). Coherence and congruence: Two aspects of personality integration. *Journal of Personality and Social Psychology, 68,* 531–543.

Sheldon, K. M., & Kasser, T. (1998). Pursuing personal goals: Skills enable progress, but not all progress is beneficial. *Personality and Social Psychology Bulletin, 24,* 1319–1331.

Sheldon, K. M., & Kasser, T. (2001). "Getting older, getting better": Personal strivings and psychological maturity across the life span. *Developmental Psychology, 37,* 491–501.

Sheldon, K. M., & McGregor, H. (2000). Extrinsic value orientation and the tragedy of the commons. *Journal of Personality, 68,* 383–411.

Sheldon, K. M., Sheldon, M. S., & Osbaldiston, R. (2000). Prosocial values and group assortation in an N-person prisoner's dilemma. *Human Nature, 11,* 387–404.

Simpson, J. B. (Ed.). (1988). *Simpson's contemporary quotations*. New York: Houghton Mifflin.

Sirgy, M. J. (1998). Materialism and quality of life. *Social Indicators Research, 43*, 227–260.

Sirgy, M. J., Cole, D., Kosenko, R., Meadow, H. L., Rahtz, D., Cicic, M., Jin, G. X., Yarsuvat, D., Blenkhorn, D. L., & Nagpal, N. (1995). A life satisfaction measure: Additional validational data for the congruity life satisfaction measure. *Social Indicators Research, 34*, 237–259.

Sirgy, M. J., Lee, D., Kosenko, R., Meadow, H. L., Rahtz, D., Cicic, M., Jin, G. X., Yarsuvat, D., Blenkhorn, D. L., & Wright, N. (1998). Does television viewership play a role in perception of quality of life? *Journal of Advertising, 27*, 125–142.

Skinner, B. F. (1972). *Beyond freedom and dignity*. New York: Alfred A. Knopf.

Solomon, S., Greenberg, J., & Pyszczynski, T. (1991). A terror management theory of social behavior: The psychological functions of self-esteem and cultural worldviews. In M. P. Zanna (Ed.), *Advances in experimental social psychology*, Vol. 24 (pp. 93–159). New York: Academic Press.

Srivastava, A., Locke, E. A., & Bortol, K. M. (2001). Money and subjective well-being: It's not the money, it's the motives. *Journal of Personality and Social Psychology, 80*, 959–971.

Stewart, A. J., & Healy, J. M. (1989). Linking individual development and social changes. *American Psychologist, 44*, 30–42.

Straus, M. A. (1979). Measuring intrafamily conflict and violence: The conflict tactics (CT) scales. *Journal of Marriage and the Family, February*, 75–88.

Strickland, E. (2001). Watch or go to jail. *Adbusters, 34*, March/April.

Swinyard, W. R., Kau, A., & Phua, H. (2001). Happiness, materialism, and religious experience in the U.S. and Singapore. *Journal of Happiness Studies, 2*, 13–32.

Tolkien, J. R. R. (1977). *The Silmarillion*. New York: Basic Books.

Vallerand, R. J. (1997). Toward a hierarchical model of intrinsic and extrinsic motivation. In M. P. Zanna (Ed.), *Advances in experimental social psychology*, Vol. 29 (pp. 271–360). New York: Academic Press.

Van de Castle, R. L. (1993). The content of dreams. In M. A. Carskadon (Ed.), *Encyclopedia of sleep and dreaming* (pp. 136–139). New York: Macmillan.

Wachtel, P. L., & Blatt, S. J. (1990). Perceptions of economic needs and of anticipated future incomes. *Journal of Economic Psychology, 11*, 403–415.

White, R. W. (1959). Motivation reconsidered: The concept of competence. *Psychological Review, 66*, 297–333.

Williams, G. C., Cox, E. M., Hedberg, V. A., & Deci, E. L. (2000). Extrinsic life goals and health risk behaviors in adolescents. *Journal of Applied Social Psychology, 30*, 1756–1771.

Winokur, J. (1996). *The rich are different*. New York: Pantheon Books.

Index